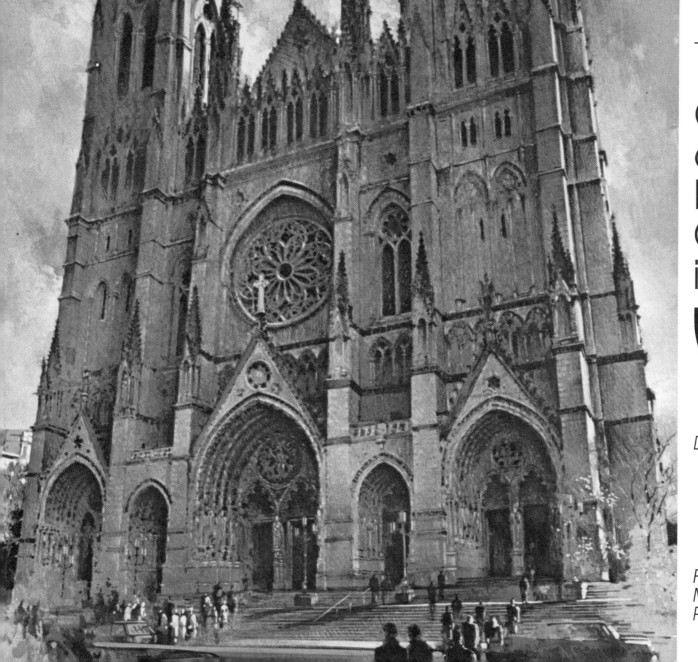

Cathedrals of the Episcopal Church in the U.S.A.

David A. Kalvelage

Forward
Movement
Publications

*To the Glory of God
In Thanksgiving
For Mary Ann*

Cover Photo—
Christ Church Cathedral,
St. Louis, Missouri

Title Page & This Page—
Cathedral of St. John the Divine,
New York City

Book Design—Barron Krody

Contents

Terms

Ambulatory—An aisle which encircles, at a lower level, an apse.

Apse—The semi-circular end of a chancel, aisle or chapel to contain an altar.

Aumbry—A receptacle, usually built into the wall of the chancel, used for keeping the reserved Sacrament.

Baptistry—The area in a church which contains a baptismal font; where baptisms take place.

Bas relief—A sculpture in which the figures project slightly from the background.

Bay—A vertical unit of division in a large church.

Bishop—A chief pastor; the head of a diocese.

Boss—An ornamental projection in vaulting.

Canon—A title granted to certain members of a cathedral staff, usually ordained.

Capital—A bell-shaped piece of masonry surmounting a pier, column or shaft.

Cathedra—The chair, seat, or throne, of a bishop.

Chancel—The area where clergy and singers are placed during services.

Chapter—The governing body of a cathedral.

Choir—The part of a cathedral in which a service is sung.

Clerestory—The windowed top story of the main structure of an aisled building.

Columbarium—A vault with spaces for urns which contain the ashes of cremated bodies.

Credence table—A table near the altar on which communion vessels are placed.

Cruciform—Shaped like a cross.

Dean—A member of the clergy in charge of a cathedral.

Flying buttress—An arch-like structure which absorbs the weight of a vault and roof, extending outside a building to the ground.

Font—A bowl-shaped object filled with water in which baptisms take place.

Gallery—The middle story of a three-story elevation.

Gothic—A style of architecture characterized by the use of pointed arches and vaulting which developed in Western Europe from the 12th century.

Grisaille—Grayish-white glass ornamented with monochrome decoration.

Hammer beam—A horizontal beam which projects from the top of a wall to carry roof braces.

Lancet window—A narrow window which terminates in a sharp point.

Lectern—A place where lessons from scripture are read; sometimes in the shape of an eagle.

Narthex—A covered porch or vestibule at the main entrance of a church.

Nave—The western arm of a church.

Polychrome—Done in several colors.

Pro-cathedral—A parish church designated by a bishop to be the host of diocesan functions.

Rector—A member of the clergy in charge of a parish church.

Reredos—An ornamental partition or screen behind an altar.

Rib—A long, curved piece of an arch.

Rood screen—An ornamental screen which serves as a partition between the nave and the choir or chancel.

Rose window—A circular window with a pattern arranged like the petals of a rose.

Sanctuary—The area around an altar.

Tabernacle—A container, usually on an altar, for consecrated bread and wine.

Transept—An arm of a cruciform church.

Truss—A framework for support of a roof.

Undercroft—A room or area underneath a church.

Vault—An arched ceiling.

Vestry—The governing body of a parish church.

Preface

Gary W. Kriss

The cathedral idea is relatively young in the Episcopal Church. The cornerstone of the first church in this country built specifically to be a cathedral was laid in 1862, and the idea was slow to take root. To this day, some American dioceses have never seen a need to establish a cathedral, and those which have done so have implemented the idea in diverse ways. Most American cathedrals, unlike their more ancient European counterparts, are parish churches as well as cathedral churches. And it would be fair to say that for most the parochial function is far more important than the cathedral function.

And yet, we continue to build cathedrals in America. Washington National Cathedral has just been completed. Work continues on the Cathedral of St. John the Divine in New York City. A new cathedral was recently completed in Fargo, North Dakota, following a fire which destroyed the old building. A new cathedral has been designated in Des Moines, Iowa, and another in Cincinnati, Ohio. The cathedral idea is apparently very much alive in the Episcopal Church.

To be sure, the shape and substance of the cathedral idea has changed over the last 130 years. It finds expression in a great variety of ways. And yet, there are some common themes. With reference to the long history and living tradition of British cathedrals, I offer here some perspectives on the role of cathedrals in the 20th and 21st centuries.

Pilgrimage

In the middle ages, cathedrals were centers of pilgrimage. Virtually every cathedral had a shrine to which pilgrims came. These shrines were dedicated to a variety of saints, some universally revered, such as Thomas Becket at Canterbury, some less well known, such as Teilo, at Llandaff in Wales. At the Reformation, the shrines were swept away and pilgrimages ended—for a time. However, pilgrimage is a fundamental motif in our faith: the journey of Abraham to a better country, the journey of Israel to the promised land, the journey of Jesus to Jerusalem to meet his destiny, and the journey of the church with her Lord on the way of the cross.

This journeying is sacramentalized in liturgical action and in actual pilgrimage. The stations of the cross were invented for the devotions of the faithful in Jerusalem. Later they became a means for those who could not make the long journey to participate in pilgrimage within their home churches. Stations continue to be a popular devotion today, and once again people are going on literal pilgrimage: to holy places, to places which constitute a center, to places which represent the end point of the journey of faith.

Cathedrals are such places. As cathedrals they are by definition centers: each is the church of a bishop whose ministry unites and focuses the ministry of a diocese. It is their place at the center of diocesan work which helps to focus just what cathedrals are about. The work of a diocese is centered in the work of its bishop, who is its chief pastor and teacher, its spiritual head. To do their work, bishops must be peripatetic, they must go out. Cathedrals, on the other hand, draw people in. In a highly mobile society such as ours, both kinds of center are important.

Daily Prayer

Prayer is the beginning and end of Christian life and, thus, of Christian pilgrimage. One thing which must be obvious to the modern visitor to British cathedrals is that they are places where the full daily round of prayer—Matins, Eucharist and Evensong—is offered, "in perpetual jubilation" as the constitution of one cathedral says. "To offer the Daily Office for ourselves and for those who do not," as one dean has put it, is what cathedrals exist for.

T.S. Eliot once wrote that a cathedral is "a kind of monastic institution open to the public." With shrinking staffs and the dispersal of clergy to live in surrounding communities, few American cathedrals even vaguely resemble monastic communities. Nevertheless, as the church of the bishop, who is the spiritual head of the diocese, cathedrals have a particular vocation to prayer, both to do the essential work of prayer and to model to the church the basic discipline of prayer. Furthermore, this daily discipline of prayer, which is found in more and more American cathedrals, forms Christian community within the cathedral staff, even if they do not live in community, and it also establishes a context for the prayers of those who come in as pilgrims.

Hospitality

Medieval cathedrals often trace their roots to even more monastic establishments which placed a high value on hospitality—welcoming pilgrims, the needy, etc. With their roots in the Benedictine monastic tradition, which emphasizes hospitality, it should not be surprising to find British cathedrals practicing an active ministry of welcome. This has become a significant ministry in the age of that secular form of pilgrimage, tourism. In many cathedrals, volunteer welcomers are stationed at the entrances during the busiest hours. Some have "chaplains" on duty; in most, vergers are always in evidence and ready to help. Visitor centers with all manners of displays, slide programs, video tapes and movies are increasingly popular and do much to encourage casual visitors to see themselves rather as pilgrims.

Not only do many cathedrals welcome those who happen to visit, but many, both in Britain and America, actively invite planned pilgrimages, particularly by parishes, deaneries and organizations from within their diocese. In Britain, as in America, cathedrals are often perceived as expensive luxuries, operating in isolation from and with indifference to the rest of the church. If cathedrals are to be taken seriously as diocesan centers, places of pilgrimage, this ministry of hospitality is essential.

Education

In 1951, T.S. Eliot described cathedrals as "the last stronghold of leisure, for the sake of scholarship and theology," referring to the substantial scholarly output of English cathedral clergy. In the ensuing years, that stronghold has suffered considerable erosion. Cathedral staffs are smaller and the demands and fast pace of modern society have changed the self-understanding even of canons in their quiet cloisters.

On the other hand, cathedrals are finding a broader educational role. Many cathedrals have committed staff and resources to developing a variety of educational programs and materials. Spend a day in a British cathedral and you are almost certain to see a school group, pens and worksheets in hand, exploring the nooks and crannies looking for carved corbels, or 12th century graffiti, or gospel stories in stained glass. In spite of the care which must be taken over the separation of church and state, American cathedrals are finding that they, too, can perform a similar function. Not only church groups, but school groups and the occasional busload of tourists are discovering the treasures of culture and tradition of which many cathedrals are the custodians.

The Arts

Rare is the British cathedral which does not have some portion of its fabric enshrouded in scaffolding. These great buildings, some resting on foundations laid before the time of William the Conqueror, are in themselves magnificent works of art and each one is rich in artistic treasures: sculpture, painting, glass, needlework, metal work and musical instruments.

Nevertheless, while art may be eternal, works of art are subject to the ravages of time, the atmosphere and human abuse. Conservation, as well as occasional restoration or replacement are employed to preserve an irreplaceable heritage. In the process, cathedrals have once again become living workshops for the practice and preservation of many of the same skills which were employed to fashion the buildings and their contents. In this country, the founding of new cathedrals as well as the designation of older buildings to be cathedrals, have sparked a similar artistic impulse. The Gothic revival has produced both good and bad imitations of ancient arts and crafts, and as confidence in the idea has grown, cathedrals have asserted themselves more and more as patrons of new arts and new artists.

Universals

By definition, cathedrals, even when they are also parish churches, transcend the parochial. Though a bishop may seldom be seen in the cathedral, it is the official seat and the cathedral represents the particular ministry of the bishop, a ministry which embodies the unity of the church and stands for the participation of the local in something larger, the church catholic. Cathedrals then have a vocation not only to stand at the center of the denominational scene, but also to foster a creative ecumenism.

Needless to say, the church does not exist for herself, but for her Lord, and for the world for which he died. Thus, it is not sufficient that the church concern herself only with "spiritual" universals. In this context, Coventry comes to mind, the cathedral which rose phoenix-like from the ashes of war and in the process gave birth to an international ministry of reconciliation, addressing such issues as post-war reconciliation with Germany, the Arab-Israeli conflict, and Ireland's social and religious divisions.

I would suggest that this last theme, "universals," is the key to understanding the vocation of cathedrals. It is axiomatic that every one of the common themes described here would or should be found in every cathedral. Nor is there any intent to suggest that this is an exhaustive list. Nothing has been said, for instance, of cathedrals as centers of mission or festivals. However, it is not the particulars which define a class. Cathedrals, by their very nature, draw us to universals. Like the bishop whose seat is in it, a cathedral is a tangible reminder that we are not Christians in isolation and that the church is not a collection of self-sufficient parishes. Rather, we are drawn into a greater unity, the church catholic, which not only incorporates the individual parts into a whole, but also gives them a center.

Gary W. Kriss is dean of Nashotah House and sometime dean of the Cathedral of All Saints, Albany, New York.

Introduction

They are as diverse as the Episcopal Church itself. They are the cathedrals of the Episcopal Church, a variable collection of buildings ranging from great Gothic structures like the famous edifices of Europe to simple parish churches. They are tied together by a bond of cathedral status which means simply that they are the bishops' churches . . . the home of the bishop's "chair" or "throne" or cathedra. It is this chair which makes a church a cathedral, a symbolic focal point of the bishop's ministry in a diocese.

The idea of cathedrals in the Episcopal Church is a relatively new one. The Episcopal Church, part of the worldwide Anglican Communion, existed in this country without cathedrals until well into the 19th century. Once the first cathedrals were established in the 1860s, the movement gathered momentum slowly, with most cathedrals originating in the early 20th century and some as recently as 1992 and 1993.

As of early 1993, there are 81 cathedrals in the Episcopal Church. Twenty dioceses have none. Some dioceses, such as Los Angeles and Rochester, once had cathedrals and now function without them. Other dioceses are studying the possibility of establishing a cathedral. At this writing, the Diocese of Western North Carolina is considering the idea of a cathedral in Asheville.

Oddly enough, three dioceses, Minnesota, Lexington and Iowa each have two cathedrals. Early in 1991, All Saints' Cathedral in the Diocese of Fort Worth voted to stop functioning as a cathedral.

Merging of dioceses have resulted in the existence of buildings now known as pro-cathedrals, as currently exist in the dioceses of the Rio Grande and Nebraska.

The Diocese of Pennsylvania established a cathedral and made plans for a great building, but it was never completed.

St. Mary's at the Cathedral exists today on the site where construction began, with only the Lady Chapel having been completed. In 1991, the diocese established The Church of the Saviour as its cathedral.

Episcopal cathedrals have existed in a railroad car, a foundry, on a mountaintop, on school campuses and various other temporary locations.

The cathedrals, while all existing as bishops' churches, have various forms of government. A few are patterned after the cathedrals of the Church of England, with a bishop, dean and chapter constituting the governing body. Most cathedrals also are parish churches and many of them function just as the typical Episcopal parish church does with a vestry as its governing body.

This book is an attempt to look briefly at Episcopal cathedrals, their histories, architecture and appointments. It examines only those cathedrals in the 50 states, but recognizes that the Episcopal Church also has cathedrals in such locations as the Virgin Islands, Puerto Rico, Haiti, Ecuador, Colombia, France, Mexico, Panama and Taiwan.

The author wishes to acknowledge the considerable assistance of deans, canons, administrators, secretaries, communications persons and historians of cathedrals in this project.

—D.K.

The author is editor of The Living Church.

The Cathedrals

Cathedral Church of St. Peter and St. Paul, Washington, DC

Pacific

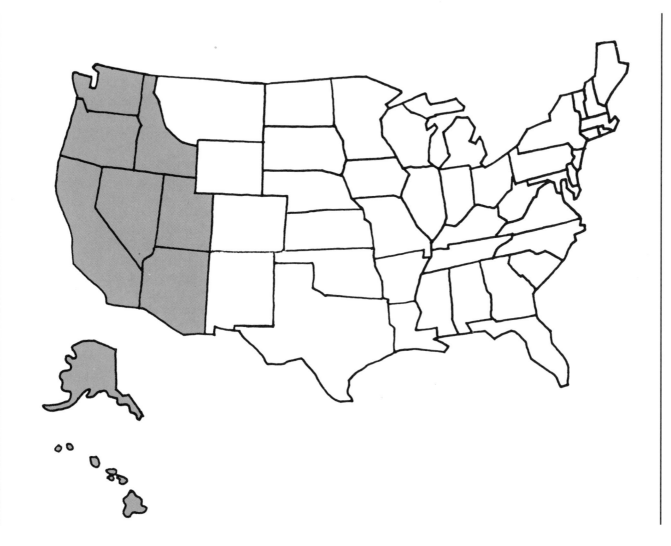

The Dioceses of

California
Arizona
El Camino Real
Hawaii
Idaho
Northern California
Olympia
Oregon
San Diego
San Joaquin
Spokane
Utah

California
Pacific

Grace Cathedral is one of the largest and best-known of Episcopal cathedrals.

This San Francisco landmark can trace its origin to 1849, when Grace Chapel was built under the leadership of John L. Ver Mehr, a Belgian-born clergyman who was the first Episcopal priest appointed to San Francisco. Grace was the second Episcopal parish in San Francisco, and most of its early communicants were miners.[1]

Two years after the construction of that first chapel, another church was built, followed by a third in 1862. William I. Kip, first Bishop of California, also served as rector of Grace Church. During that time of dual ministry, Grace Church took on an unofficial designation of cathedral.

William F. Nichols, who was Bishop Kip's successor, spoke as early as 1892 of the possibility of a diocesan cathedral on one of San Francisco's hilltops.[2] The Nob Hill area, where Grace Church was located, seemed ideally suited.

In 1906, when the great earthquake devastated the city, Grace Church was ruined by the fire which followed the tragedy. The Crocker family, who lived on Nob Hill, had its homes destroyed by the fire, and family members donated their ruined block to the diocese as a site for a cathedral. A temporary building, known as Grace Pro-Cathedral, was constructed in 1907 and served as the cathedral until 1914. In 1910, the cornerstone for a new cathedral, to be designed by English architect G.F. Bodley, was dedicated by Bishop Nichols, but no further construction took place. Grace Parish was dissolved at that time.

Cathedral House, which is the administration center, was built in 1912. The design of the planned cathedral was changed and used for the construction of the Founders Crypt, the basement level of the cathedral, which was completed in 1914

and served as the cathedral for 17 years. Founders Crypt was not used in the present building with the exception of the entrance portal.

Preparation for construction of the present cathedral began in 1925 under the direction of Lewis P. Hobart as architect and Ralph Adams Cram as consultant. Construction started in 1928, beginning with the Chapel of Grace. Work continued on the choir, transepts and crossing despite the Great Depression. There was a lull in construction early in 1931, but work soon continued on the nave and aisles. Construction was completed to the third bay by 1933 and a temporary enclosing wall was built. The north tower, which contains the carillon, was built from 1936-41, then no further construction took place for nearly 20 years.

In 1961, following a golden anniversary fund drive, construction resumed. The building, largely completed, was consecrated November 20, 1964.

Grace Cathedral's design is largely late 12th and 13th century French Gothic. It is built of concrete and steel, with foundations resting on sheared sandstone and shale bedrock. The building faces west, rather than the traditional east, to avoid prevailing west winds and to face downtown.

Upon entering the cathedral from the east porch, one sees the baptismal font, designed by Hans and Norman Grag in 1964. The font is of brass/bronze and aluminum and rests on steps of granite from Scotland, New England and California, representing the transition of the episcopate. The nave has a floor of Indiana limestone and oak. The pews also are of oak and are backed by chairs from the Founders Crypt which were used in 1914.

The high altar is located in the crossing and is made of five blocks of California granite topped by California redwood.

The altar was installed in 1964; previously, the cathedral's altar was located in the apse. The carved pulpit was installed in 1942 and the contemporary lectern in 1968. The sanctuary communion rails are of Roman travertine marble.

The carved cathedra in the apse dates from 1937 and was designed by Lewis Hobart. The Gothic-style clergy and choir stalls along the choir walls were installed in 1949.

Both transepts contain a series of flags, installed in 1976 during the nation's bicentennial observance. Flags in the north transept are from colonial and revolutionary America, and those in the south transept are devoted to California history.

Grace Cathedral has some brilliantly-colored stained glass windows. Among them is the rose window at the east end by the Gabriel Loire Studios of Chartres, France. Installed in 1964, it illustrates St. Francis' Canticle of the Sun and contains nearly 3,800 pieces of glass. The first three window groups in both the south and north aisles are by the Henry L. Willet Studios of Philadelphia. They date from 1966 and portray various reforms. Other windows in both aisles are by the Charles J. Connick Studios of Boston and depict fruits of the Spirit.

The nave clerestory features the human endeavor windows by Loire, which depict such well-known persons as Frank Lloyd Wright, Henry Ford and John Glenn.

Both aisles contain murals. Polish-American artist John H. DeRosen did those in the south aisle, which depict world church leaders. Along the north aisle are murals by Antonio Sotomayor portraying events in the history of Grace Parish and Cathedral.

Other windows of note by Connick are found in both transepts. In the south are windows depicting the New Testament and Psalm 23. The north transept contains an Old Testament window. Windows in the apse and choir clerestory have as their theme the mystical Nine Choirs of Angels from Dionysian theology, and also are by Connick.

The Chapel of Grace, used for daily services, contains an altar from the French chateau of Sigournais, which dates from about 1430, and a three-paneled oak reredos made in Flanders in about 1490. Outside the chapel is a 13th century crucifix from the Barcelona region of Spain. Nearby, in the south choir aisle, is a tapestry made in Brussels about 1530.

The Chapel of the Nativity, off the north transept, includes a renaissance painting of the Madonna and Child, and a mural of the adoration.

The cathedral's organ is an Aeolian-Skinner installed in 1934. With recent additions and improvements, it contains 123 ranks and 7,286 pipes.

In 1991, plans were made to begin an $11 million capital campaign which will complete the original architectural plan by removing the existing Cathedral House and construct a grand stairway leading up to the front of the cathedral.[3]

Trinity Cathedral, Phoenix

Arizona
Pacific

After a 73-year existence as a pro-cathedral, Trinity was designated as the cathedral of the Diocese of Arizona in 1988 by the Rt. Rev. Joseph Heistand.

Episcopal services were held in Phoenix as early as the spring of 1882, when George K. Dunlop, Bishop of the Missionary District of Arizona and New Mexico, came to that community. Services were held in various places, including a Baptist church, a Methodist church and Pythian Hall, for the next few years.

In 1885, a meeting was held to organize a congregation, and a lot was purchased the following year. The cornerstone for the first Trinity Church was laid on Trinity Sunday, May 27, 1888, and the first service in the new brick building was on the Feast of the Epiphany, January 6, 1889.

Trinity was organized as a parish in 1907, three years before Arizona became a separate missionary district, apart from New Mexico. In 1911, Julius W. Atwood, bishop of the new missionary district, established Trinity as the pro-cathedral. Later that year, the lot on which the present cathedral stands was purchased.

Plans for a new church were made, and in 1915 construction began on the present complex. The cornerstone for Cathedral House was laid October 31, 1915, and services were moved from the old church to the auditorium of the new building on Christmas Day, 1915.

Construction of the new church began in the summer of 1920, and the first service was held on Christmas Day of that year. The building was consecrated April 1, 1921. The cathedral was designed in Spanish colonial style and is patterned after a building in Majorca, Spain.[4]

The cornerstone for Bishop Atwood Hall, the third side of the quadrangle which forms the cathedral close, was laid December 28, 1930, and the building was completed the following spring.

Some major renovations of the buildings have taken place in recent years. Cathedral House and Atwood Hall were renovated in 1973-75, and the cathedral itself underwent considerable changes beginning in 1984. Following Christmas services that year, services were moved out of the church, and the congregation went back into the cathedral at Christmas, 1986. During that renovation, the nave was reversed, with worshipers now facing south rather than north.

The cathedral's entry doors of wrought iron grillwork were designed by Glidden Parker, of the Glassart Studio in Scottsdale, Arizona. Parker also was the designer of the stained glass windows, which were executed and installed in 1966-67.

The windows are unusual in that winged forms expressing the Trinity are found in each of them.[5] A rose window is found at the south end of the building, dominated by triangles which symbolize the Trinity. The rose window was the first one designed, although the window in the baptistry was the first installed. The balcony window illustrates New Testament faith, the choir window depicts the music of worship, and some of the nave windows show grace, creation, man's life being entered by God, man responding to God's intervention, man's earthly struggle, and the Resurrection.

A service officially marking Trinity's status as the cathedral was held June 16, 1991, with Bishop Heistand officiating.[6]

Later in 1991, The Episcopal Church held its General Convention in Phoenix, and the cathedral had many distinguished visitors, including the church's Presiding Bishop, Edmond Browning.

El Camino Real
Pacific

Trinity Cathedral serves one of the fastest-growing areas of California, one of the nation's most rapidly-growing states. It has been a cathedral only since 1989 and its diocese also is young, having existed since 1980.

San Jose has had Episcopal ministry ever since 1854, when William I. Kip, Missionary Bishop of California, held a service in May of that year in a Presbyterian church. Following that event, a group of nine met frequently, sometimes in homes and occasionally in the Presbyterian church.[7] There was enough growth to call a resident priest in 1860. He held services in a firehouse, and in the following year, the little congregation moved to a permanent location, the second story of a building which was used as a courtroom.

The parish was organized February 22, 1861. Construction soon began on a wooden church building, which was ready for occupancy on Advent Sunday, 1863. That made Trinity the oldest church building in continuous use in San Jose. The church was consecrated July 27, 1867, by Bishop Kip.

Extensive remodeling and enlargement took place in the 1870s. The old building was divided, half of it to serve as the south transept of the enlarged church, and the other half as the new nave. The church was reopened by Bishop Kip September 3, 1876. A bell tower was added about 1880.

Eight years later, a parish house was constructed, and a second floor and chapel were added in 1931. A Youth Center building was constructed in 1949, providing space for offices, a library and other rooms.

There was extensive reconstruction in 1958, including structural reinforcement, enlargement of the patio entrance and choir section, and the refitting and modernization of some rooms. Trinity's organ also was renovated. The building was rededicated by the Rt. Rev. James Pike November 16, 1958.

During its first 119 years, Trinity was part of the Diocese of California. In 1980, the Diocese of El Camino Real was created and San Jose became its see city. Trinity became a cathedral June 18, 1989, under C. Shannon Mallory, who was beginning the final year of his episcopate.[8]

Some of Trinity's windows have been in place since the original building opened in 1863. Perhaps the most unusual window in the cathedral, and probably the oldest, is the Ascension window above the entrance. It is made of enameled glass, which was a process used for only a short time in Germany during the 1700s. The glass apparently was imported from Germany by the Thomas Schneider Studios of New York City and once was part of the Church of the Holy Saviour in Santa Clara, California, before being moved to San Jose.[9]

Some of the earliest windows came from studios in the East. The original 18 were shipped around Cape Horn by sailing vessel. Most of those can be identified by a light brown pattern that fills the background and by the fact that they are painted rather than stained.

Other windows of interest are the large triple window, one of the originals, which was moved to its current location behind the altar, and the eight trefoil clerestory windows.

The cathedral organ was purchased from Trinity Church, San Francisco, in 1924.

When the bell tower was constructed in 1880, it contained five bells, which were believed to compose the oldest chime on the West Coast.[10] Two more were added in 1905, another two in 1960, and nine more in 1976.

Hawaii
Pacific

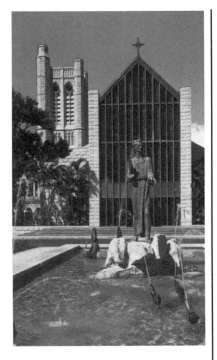

The royal family of Hawaii was closely involved in the founding of St. Andrew's Cathedral. The cathedral is one of the oldest in the American Church, and is a rare American example of early French Gothic architecture.

King Kamehameha IV, who had come to the Hawaiian throne in 1854, was no stranger to Anglicanism. He had attended Anglican services in England and the United States, and in 1858, he and Queen Emma began a movement to found an Anglican church in Hawaii. Inquiries were made in England and the United States about the possibility of sending clergy to Hawaii. Because of the impending Civil War in the United States, efforts were more successful in England.

In 1861, Thomas Staley was consecrated in London as Bishop of Hawaii, and the following year, he, two priests and their families, arrived in Hawaii. The king offered land for a church, and Queen Emma was baptized soon after Bishop Staley's arrival. A few weeks later, both the king and queen were confirmed.

A congregation was formed and a wooden structure built for worship, which soon became known as a pro-cathedral.

On November 30, 1863, St. Andrew's Day, King Kamehameha died. The king, who had been working on a translation of the Book of Common Prayer into Hawaiian, was succeeded on the throne by his brother, Kamehameha V.

Two years later, Queen Emma traveled to England to raise funds for construction of a cathedral. She also secured architectural plans.

The cornerstone for the cathedral was laid March 5, 1867 by Kamehameha V. It was named St. Andrew's in commemoration of the day Kamehameha IV had died. Work began on the foundation and the choir section, but it stopped in 1870 when Bishop Staley returned to England. Work resumed in 1882, and on Christmas Day, 1886, the choir was completed and used for worship.

The building was consecrated in 1902 even though it was far from completed. Only a portion of the nave was finished. Later that year, the Bishop of California visited Hawaii and received the Anglican Church of Hawaii into the Episcopal Church. Hawaii had been annexed as an American territory in 1898.

Work continued on an irregular basis, and it took 50 years to complete the cathedral. On September 21, 1958, two bays, pews, narthex, vestibules and the great west window were consecrated.

Today the cathedral stands in a lovely setting in downtown Honolulu. An unusual fountain attracts the attention as a visitor approaches the cathedral. The fountain is dominated by a statue of St. Andrew.

The entire entrance to the cathedral, with the exception of the brass doors, is made up of the great west window. The brilliant wall of stained glass is one of the largest ever constructed in the United States, and is about 50 feet high and 20 feet wide. It was designed by John Wallis in 1956, and contains glass handblown in France, Germany, Belgium, England and the United States. The central panel symbolizes the Trinity and the gospel, the left panel depicts the life of Christ, the right panel portrays the spread of the faith, and the bottom is devoted to the church in Hawaii.

Inside, St. Andrew's is a fine example of Gothic architecture with massive columns and vaulting. The high altar is constructed largely of stone, from near Caen in Normandy, and was dedicated in 1908.

The baptismal font is one of the oldest appointments in St. Andrew's. It was sent from England in 1862.

Idaho
Pacific

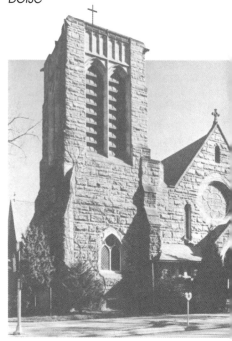

Not only is Idaho's cathedral the only one in the Episcopal Church named St. Michael's, it appears to be the only one named for its founder, who began his ministry in a log hut with a dirt floor.

The Rev. St. Michael Fackler, a missionary in Oregon for 17 years, held the first Episcopal service in Boise in August, 1864, in that modest building. A congregation was organized and had its first church building by 1866, a building which still stands and is now in its third location. That church was named St. Michael's August 29, 1867, following the death of Fackler, who was stricken on his way east aboard a ship.

Daniel Tuttle, missionary bishop in the Northwest, visited St. Michael's in October, 1867, and was instrumental in organizing a parish school. Bishop Tuttle assisted workers who added a wing to the church in 1869, and he consecrated the frame building October 12, 1873.

Bishop Tuttle's successor, Ethelbert Talbot, became Bishop of Wyoming and Idaho in 1886 and soon formed St. Margaret's Girls School, which functioned for many years. The school was reorganized as a junior college for girls in 1933, and became Boise Junior College in 1939.

Bishop Talbot chose Laramie, Wyoming, as his see city, although he had been invited to Boise. When James B. Funsten was consecrated as Bishop of Idaho in 1899, Boise became the see city and plans soon were made for a cathedral.

On September 7, 1899, ground was broken for a cathedral on land that was formerly an orchard. The basement was completed during the winter of 1899, and by 1901, work had begun on the interior. The present cathedral building was dedicated May 25, 1902. The old church was moved to a new location.

The new St. Michael's is English Gothic in design with the walls of sandstone from Table Rock. When the building was dedicated, many of the furnishings had not been obtained and the windows were of plain opaque glass. The ceiling is mostly of pine and fir. The main woodwork is plain and quarter-sawed oak and the tresses are of Idaho pine.

Entrance to the cathedral is through the bell tower, which was built in 1961 as a memorial to service personnel killed during World War II. The stone baptismal font was brought from the first St. Michael's and dates to 1869. A series of 12 interesting windows known as the Apostles' Windows form a gateway from the narthex to the nave and contain shields of the apostles.

The windows in the nave are the oldest type of stained glass windows in the cathedral. They portray familiar stories from the Old Testament, and their designer is unknown.

The Nativity (south) transept is the most recent addition to St. Michael's, having been constructed in 1976. The transept contains a Tiffany window depicting the Nativity which is comprised of three lancets. Included in this transept is a stone near the door which is a gift from Washington Cathedral.

The north transept contains the Chapel of the Resurrection. Three windows created by Charles J. Connick of Boston have a theme of Resurrection.

Seven lancet-shaped windows are found at the east end of the cathedral. Five of them, beginning at the left, were designed by Connick. The other two are original apse windows donated by the Daughters of the King.

The rose window at the back of the church also was designed by Connick and was dedicated in 1945.

In 1992, plans were made to do additional refurbishing and remodeling. In the same year, St. Michael's garden columbarium was dedicated.

Northern California
Pacific

Sacramento's cathedral is one of the newer buildings among Episcopal cathedrals, having been consecrated in 1955.

Trinity Mission was established in 1898. A church was constructed in 1900 next to the residence of William Hall Moreland, Bishop of the Missionary District of Northern California. Bishop Moreland hoped to build a large, Gothic cathedral, but his plans never materialized.[11]

Trinity was designated as a pro-cathedral in 1910, but two years later most of its members signed a petition requesting the church be granted parish status. Bishop Moreland refused to grant the request and created a situation in which many resigned membership.[12] The church was incorporated as Trinity Cathedral Church in 1913.

An odd situation existed in 1934, when the cathedral had two deans. When both Trinity and St. Paul's Church were beset by financial problems, Bishop A.W. Noel Porter merged the two, designating St. Paul's as Christ Church Cathedral. The clergy from each church were appointed as deans, serving on alternate Sundays, with the bishop officiating when there was a fifth Sunday of the month.[13]

Trinity's small wooden building became known as the Bishop's Chapel. It was renovated in 1937 and became a center for servicemen and their families during World War II.

In 1945, Trinity became a parish, and three years later it returned to pro-cathedral status.

The present cathedral, a brick building with a distinctive spire, was dedicated October 23, 1955, following years of rapid growth by both the community and the congregation.

Cathedral House was built in 1909 with donations from a family in the East, and used until the 1960s, when it was replaced by the present Cathedral House, a site for Christian education, fellowship and a center for outreach ministries, in 1968.

During the years following the completion of the present cathedral building, Trinity's congregation was burdened by a large financial debt, but continued growth enabled that obstacle to be overcome, and great progress took place during the 1980s. The interior was renovated, stained glass windows added to the nave, the sanctuary enlarged and a new pipe organ was installed.

Most visitors to Trinity enter through the narthex doors, which contain panels of stained glass depicting faith, courage and service. The glass also depicts Bishop Kip, the first Missionary Bishop of California, astronaut Neil Armstrong on the Moon, Albert Schweitzer ministering in Africa, and Jane Hull caring for the disadvantaged.

Trinity's nave has six stained glass windows on each side, which were made by a process in which each piece of glass was chipped and set in a cement base. The windows on the left side illustrate miracles of Jesus. Those on the right side depict parables told by Jesus. The bottom third of each of the nave windows shows various aspects of life in Northern California, including gold mining, wine making and the completion of the railroad.

Trinity's large sanctuary is highlighted by a reredos behind a free-standing altar. The reredos contains a simple wooden cross made by a member of the parish. The window above the altar has a brilliant blue background and portrays the lamb of God.

At the other end of the building, above the organ's imperial trumpets, is a small, round window from the old cathedral showing a chalice and a host.

Olympia
Pacific

St. Mark's has one of the most unusual histories and one of the most unusual buildings among Episcopal cathedrals. The building is unfinished, went through foreclosure and served as a training center for the United States Army during World War II.

St. Mark's was the second parish founded in Seattle, having been organized in 1889. A temporary parish house was built at once and dedicated February 16, 1890. That building served as the worship center for the congregation until it moved to a new location in 1896. An English-style church was built and the parish prospered into the 20th century.

The site for the present cathedral was acquired in 1923, and plans were made to construct a large cathedral, "intended to be the greatest neo-Gothic cathedral on the Pacific Rim." S. Arthur Huston, second Bishop of Olympia, designated St. Mark's as the cathedral in 1926.

The cornerstone was laid in 1930, and the uncompleted building was opened for worship April 26, 1931, but troubles followed almost immediately. Because of the depression, income dropped rapidly and the congregation faced a $250,000 mortgage and a building which was far from completion. When money ran out, the building was capped as inexpensively as possible with unfinished fir and the concrete and steel pillars enclosed with wood and plaster.

After the church struggled financially for the next decade, a bonding company foreclosed on the mortgage and the doors of the cathedral were locked. A for sale sign appeared but there were no takers. The Army took over the building in 1943, and used it as a training center for an anti-aircraft unit. During this period the congregation dwindled, but never gave up. Services and church school were held at a country club and in St. Barnabas' Chapel.

When World War II ended, in 1945, the building was reopened and the congregation was given two years to meet the mortgage. Members of St. Mark's and other Episcopalians were able to raise about half the money needed to meet the mortgage, and the bonding company reduced the mortgage and forgave the interest, enabling St. Mark's members to look to the future.

One of the first sights greeting members when they returned to the church was the black-out paint on the windows which had been applied by the Army.

Plans to finish the cathedral were discussed in 1953-54, and by 1957 a general building scheme was approved which would involve no major additions to the church building with the exception of an apse.

A new sanctuary area was completed in July, 1967, incorporating the former choir and sanctuary in a single setting for the altar as the focus of worship.

The concrete structure which is St. Mark's today is only the interior foundation of what was planned as the great neo-Gothic building. The current building was to have been the base for a lantern tower rising some 200 feet. The original design featured a short nave and apse, and the exterior was to be faced with Wilkinson stone.

When St. Mark's observed its centennial in 1989, a Century II plan was formed, which would raise $12.15 million for renovation and expansion of the cathedral and provide a new building for education and administration. The plan would provide for the completion of the cathedral, including extension of the narthex, opening interior space, installation of flooring, finishing and painting of walls and installation of windows. By late 1990, the campaign had raised more than a million dollars and is proceeding.

*Cathedral of
St. John the Baptist,
Portland*

Oregon

Pacific

The modern building in suburban Portland is the second cathedral the Diocese of Oregon has had, replacing a downtown church in 1973.

Much of the early work of the Episcopal Church in Oregon was accomplished by Thomas F. Scott, who arrived in April, 1854, after being chosen the first Missionary Bishop for the Oregon Country. That territory included the states of Oregon and Washington and parts of what later became Idaho. Bishop Scott founded local congregations and a school for boys in the Beaverton area during his 13-year episcopate.

His successor, Benjamin W. Morris, also emphasized education, and founded St. Helen's Hall for girls in 1870. He traveled widely for 36 years, but had no church of his own. Following his death in 1906, the cathedral idea came to Portland with the election of Bishop Charles Scadding, who had been dean of the cathedral in Chicago. By this time, Oregon was a diocese of its own, but Bishop Scadding died in 1915 before his idea became a reality.

Scadding's successor, Walter T. Sumner, used Trinity Church in downtown Portland much like a cathedral without designating it officially.[14]

Meanwhile, St. Stephen's Church, organized in 1863, evolved into a cathedral. St. Stephen's was known as a chapel in its early days, then as a pro-cathedral, and in 1928 it was incorporated as a cathedral.[15]

Following the death of Bishop Benjamin D. Dagwell in 1958, a school for boys was erected next to St. Helen's School. The two are now known as the Oregon Episcopal Schools.

The present cathedral had beginnings in St. Stephen's Chapel. That small congregation, affiliated with St. Stephen's Cathedral, held its first service October 4, 1964, in a recreation room of the Oregon Episcopal Schools. Services continued the following year with school students in attendance, and in 1966, ground was broken for a chapel building. The new chapel was in use in time for Holy Week, 1967. Meanwhile construction continued and memorial gifts were received.

When the Diocese of Oregon held its convention in 1973, the church on the school campus was recognized as the Cathedral Church of St. John the Baptist, and St. Stephen's Cathedral became St. Stephen's Parish.

The contemporary building was designed by Lewis Crutcher and Charles E. Johnson. The sanctuary furniture was designed by Roger Sogge and the stained glass by Albert A. Gerlach. The organ, made by the D.A. Flentrop firm of Zandaam, Holland, was installed in 1972.

By 1993, it appeared as though the Diocese of Oregon would soon have its third cathedral of the 20th century. The diocesan convention and Bishop Robert Ladehoff decided that the larger Trinity Church in downtown Portland would be a more suitable cathedral. Trinity, the home of the largest congregation in the diocese, began to plan for the transition.

San Diego
Pacific

The congregation which worships in the beautiful Gothic cathedral in southern California can trace its origin to a little church named Holy Trinity.

Episcopal services were held in San Diego as early as July 10, 1853, when Army Chaplain John Reynolds held the first non-Roman Catholic service in San Diego, which also was the first Episcopal service in Southern California.[16] Services were held irregularly in a variety of places for a time, and a mission named Holy Trinity was organized December 18, 1869. That congregation soon had its own all-purpose building called Trinity Hall, which opened for services May 30, 1870. The hall was moved to a new location 11 months later.

In 1885, Holy Trinity became known as St. Paul's, and the following year lots were purchased for a new, larger church. A new building was ready for services on Easter Day, April 10, 1887.

St. Paul's had been part of the Diocese of California since its organization, but when the Diocese of Los Angeles was formed December 3, 1895, St. Paul's became part of the new jurisdiction. The church was consecrated March 9, 1902, by Joseph H. Johnson, first Bishop of Los Angeles.

The parish showed steady growth, bringing about an enlargement in 1912, which increased seating capacity by 50 percent. In 1919, the parish purchased the site of the present cathedral, and the vestry hired the architectural firm of Frohman, Robb and Little, architect of Washington Cathedral, to design a new complex.

A large financial campaign led to the formation of a three-stage building plan. Ground was broken January 3, 1928, for a parish house, which represented phase one of the project. The building was ready for occupancy that year and dedicated December 30, 1928.

Phase two, the building of the present cathedral, began in 1947 when the vestry contacted Philip H. Frohman with the intention of "constructing at least a part of a new church."[17] The congregation moved out of its church building May 16, 1948, and held services in the parish house for three and a half years.

The cornerstone of the new church was laid April 4, 1951, by the Rt. Rev. Francis E. Bloy, and construction moved so quickly that the first service was held December 2 of that year. The church was consecrated December 8, 1951.

Rapid growth in Southern California led to the formation of the Diocese of San Diego in 1974. From the earliest days of the new diocese, St. Paul's functioned much like a cathedral, including the location of the bishop's office there. Cathedral status was achieved in 1985 under C. Brinkley Morton, second Bishop of San Diego.

When St. Paul's became the cathedral, renovations were made in the sanctuary. The bishop's chair was constructed from carved portions of pews in the choir area, which had been removed in the renovation, and the cathedra was placed at the east end of the building, with a wooden banner affixed with the diocesan coat of arms behind it.

The altar was moved forward from the east end, and a cross hung above it. The brilliantly-colored cross is both Gothic in design to match the present building and contemporary to emphasize that the Lord reigns in people's lives.[18]

The cathedral's stained glass windows were executed by the Judson Studios of South Pasadena, California. The clerestory windows in the nave depict important persons from Abraham and Moses to the first Bishop of California. Windows along the nave aisle portray stories from the life of St. Paul.

*St. James' Cathedral,
Fresno*

San Joaquin
Pacific

The congregation of St. James' Cathedral has overcome an earthquake and the condemnation of its building, and now worships in "temporary" quarters.

St. James' was organized in 1879 by the Rev. D.O. Kelley, who held services in a law office, then in an old garret for several months, and finally in a public school. In 1880, the congregation made plans for its own building. Occasional services had been held in Fresno before 1879 by priests traveling through the San Joaquin Valley.

The first service in the new church was held in the spring of 1881, even though the building had not been completed. At that time, it consisted of little more than bare brick walls, a roof, floor and windows.

The church was not finished or cleared of debt until December 7, 1884, when it was consecrated by Bishop William I. Kip of the Diocese of California. The mission achieved parish status in 1888.

That church was demolished and on September 8, 1901, the cornerstone was laid for a new edifice. The new church and a rectory were completed in 1902.

When the Missionary District of San Joaquin was created out of the Diocese of California in 1910, Fresno became the see city. Louis C. Sanford became first bishop of the missionary district and worked out an agreement with the vestry of St. James', establishing it as a pro-cathedral. The event marked the realization of the dream of the parish's founder 40 years earlier. The pro-cathedral was consecrated October 27, 1911, and it became a full cathedral in 1925.

Sumner Walters, who succeeded Bishop Sanford, did not always have a cordial relationship with St. James' and for a time made St. John's, Stockton, "his" church, while St. James' continued to have the title of cathedral church.

Sanford Hall was erected in 1951 as a parish hall. Five years later, the great Central Valley earthquake struck Fresno and caused severe structural damage to the church. It was deemed unsafe for occupancy and condemned by city inspectors. Services were moved to the parish hall April 1, 1957.

The cathedral chapter purchased a site for a new building, but that site proved to be unsuitable when it was learned the property was under the flight path for the new Fresno air terminal. The problem was solved when a local dairyman traded his property (the location of the present cathedral) for the site acquired by the chapter.

The present facilities, erected as an all-purpose building, were built in 1960. Future development of the property and facilities is in abeyance.

St. James' contains an interesting high altar, carved by the Rev. Canon Frederick Graves and finished in 1938. The colorful figures carved into the front of the wooden altar represent the angels who ministered to Jesus during his life on earth. When the altar was dedicated in 1938, the carved Good Shepherd pulpit also was dedicated. The pulpit was made in England for St. Stephen's, San Francisco (where Bishop Walters had been rector), about 1896. When St. Stephen's was closed, the pulpit was put into storage and later donated to St. James'. The pulpit had been painted gray, but has been restored to its natural state.

Some stained glass windows from earlier buildings remain in the cathedral. The lancet windows now in the back of the building have been refinished, and some other early windows are found in the narthex. A large window which had been behind the altar in the old church remains in storage.

In 1989, some renovation of facilities took place, including the installation of pew-chair seating.

Spokane
Pacific

Spokane's splendid Gothic cathedral is the result of some far-reaching vision by one of its earliest bishops.

When Edward Cross was appointed to the Far West Missionary District in 1923, the decision already had been made to replace All Saints' Cathedral in Spokane. The aging, frame building, which had opened in 1891, was in poor physical condition and was not of the size needed to be the center of diocesan ministry.

Bishop Cross had grand ideas for a new cathedral. In a newspaper article dated August 31, 1926, he said, "We need to do something outstanding to enthrone God in the hearts of men."[19]

His vision was to follow in the traditions of the great cathedrals of Washington and New York, an ecumenical ministry which would serve the entire community.

Bishop Cross's plan began with a successful two-week fund-raising drive which brought in $200,000.

Harold C. Whitehouse of Spokane, a parishioner, was selected as the architect and toured Europe, studying the details of Gothic buildings.

Construction began in 1925, and the $200,000 estimate soon became $400,000.

On October 20, 1929, three Spokane parishes were merged into one cathedral congregation. All Saints, St. Peter's and St. James' churches were the forerunners of St. John's, and celebrated on that date the dedication of the completed first unit of the new building, which included the nave and the base of the tower. Nine days later, the stock market crashed, and construction was halted for 19 years.

Even though construction ceased and debts from a mortgage plagued St. John's, the congregation grew during this period, and by the 1950s showed 3,600 members.[20]

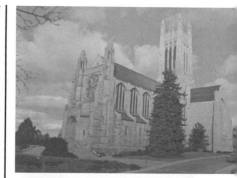

Construction began again in 1948, with the Spokane firm of Henry George and Sons building the chancel, sanctuary, transepts and tower over a six-year period.

The building is of English Gothic design, but its details include the French influence. The outer structure is solid stone using materials quarried near Tacoma. Sandstone from Idaho makes up the interior of the nave, and the rest of the interior is made from Indiana limestone.

The nave is typically Gothic with ribbed vaulting and pointed arches. The beams of the ceiling are of solid California redwood. The four main arches at the crossing have four symbols of the church: a ship, the Ark of the Covenant, a candlestick and a house on a rock.

The cathedral foundation stone is found in the northeast pier of the tower. It was set in place June 10, 1928, by Bishop Lemuel H. Wells. It contains stones from the Mount of Olives, Glastonbury Abbey, the first Episcopal Church in Jamestown, Virginia, and the former All Saints' Cathedral in Spokane.

The high altar was crafted in Italy of Carrara marble. Behind it, the reredos is of limestone, carved by Arcangelo Cascieri of Boston.

Most of the stained glass windows were created by Charles J. Connick and Associates of Boston. The trefoil window above the reredos honors the Holy Trinity. Clerestory windows in the chancel depict prominent events in the life of Jesus. The small windows along the side aisles portray the developing life of the church. Three windows, designed by the Willet Studio and depicting the Crucifixion, Resurrection and Ascension, were added to the upper south side chancel in 1992.

St. Mark's Cathedral, Salt Lake City

Utah
Pacific

St. Mark's Cathedral, although one of the smallest, is one of the oldest in the Episcopal Church.

Daniel S. Tuttle, Missionary Bishop of the Northwest, who was instrumental in the founding of several American cathedrals, had a major role in this one. He wrote that it would not be appropriate to copy the English model for cathedrals, but that "the cathedral is to be developed along lines adapted to American ideas and adjusted to American habits."[21]

The cornerstone for St. Mark's was laid July 30, 1870, by Bishop Tuttle, and the church became the first building in Utah to house a non-Mormon congregation. Blueprints were donated by well-known church architect Richard Upjohn, and contributions were received from Philadelphia and New York in hopes of combatting polygamy in Utah.[22]

A congregation was organized November 15, 1870, and services were held in Independence Hall in Salt Lake City. Services were moved to the new building May 21, 1871, with the congregation worshiping in a small chapel in the crypt. Services were moved to the nave September 3, 1871, and the building was consecrated as a cathedral May 14, 1874.

Upjohn's design was a traditional cruciform shape, constructed of thick, sandstone walls and heavy, timber roof trusses. Its capacity was only 500 persons, but at that time it would accommodate every Episcopalian in the territory.

The cathedral soon became the center of Bishop Tuttle's ministry, as St. Mark's School, Rowland Hall School and St. Mark's Hospital all were operating by 1880.

A chancel and sanctuary were added in 1901, but that area was destroyed in 1935 when fire struck the building. The fire started in a basement furnace and caused heavy damage to the floor, ceiling and stained glass windows. Among the losses were two Tiffany windows over the altar. The church was restored with only minor modification, and used again on Passion Sunday, 1936.

A major renovation took place in 1988-89. The crumbling foundation was repaired, the lower level was improved, the floor and lighting system were refurbished, and the narthex remodeled.

The altar, the center of St. Mark's worship, is freestanding, backed by a walnut reredos, which was installed following the fire. The reredos contains carvings of four saints of the Anglican Communion, including Alban and Thomas Becket.

Nearby is the bishop's cathedra, also of walnut, which was not damaged in the fire. It was brought to Salt Lake City from a ship which had to sail around Cape Horn to reach the Pacific Coast. The sanctuary floor is of Montana travertine. A bronze plaque commemorates Bishop Tuttle.

On the wall to the right as one enters the chancel is a composite carving of Stations of the Cross executed by Utah sculptor Peter Chase.

The east transept contains the baptistry, which has a marble font, and an icon of the Blessed Virgin Mary on the door of the aumbry.

Among the cathedral windows are two of Tiffany-style on both sides of the altar which depict the Resurrection. A Tiffany window in the west wall of the nave is a rendition of the Annunciation. The two windows in the west wall of the chapel are by the Connick Studio and represent the Crucifixion and the Last Supper. On the south wall, the window showing the Palm Sunday entry into Jerusalem was made by William Littig of Salt Lake City. A rose window is found high on the wall of both transepts.

East

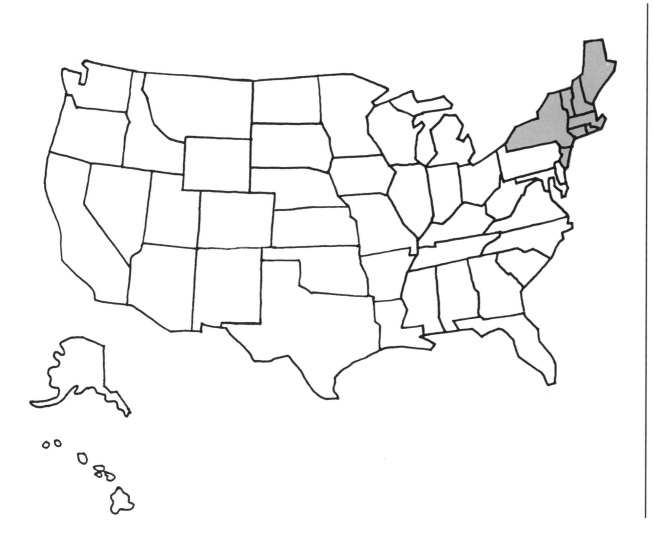

The Dioceses of

New York
Albany
Central New York
Connecticut
Long Island
Maine
Massachusetts
New Jersey
Newark
Rhode Island
Vermont
Western Massachusetts
Western New York

New York

East

The Cathedral of St. John the Divine is the largest cathedral in the world, occupying 121,000 square feet with a length of more than 600 feet, and it is the second largest church in the world. The only one larger is St. Peter's, Rome, which is a basilica, not a cathedral. As of this writing, St. John's is unfinished, with the west towers and the transepts and crossing to be completed.

The idea of a cathedral in the nation's largest city was mentioned as early as 1828, according to the diary of one-time mayor Philip Howe, who said Bishop John Henry Hobart spoke to him about the possibility.[1]

No action toward the building of a cathedral took place until 1872, when Bishop Horatio Potter proposed the idea to the diocesan convention, which approved. A charter for a cathedral was granted in 1873, but a financial panic late that year delayed plans.

A site was chosen in 1887, and a design contest was held the following year with 60 architects entered. The design of Heins and LaFarge of New York City was chosen.

On the Feast of St. John, December 27, 1892, the cornerstone was laid by Bishop Henry C. Potter, nephew of the previous bishop. A crypt chapel was in use by 1899, and the choir and crossing were consecrated April 19, 1911. From that point until 1938, the cathedral consisted of the choir area and the temporary structure within the four arches of the crossing.[2]

A change in architects was made following the death of Heins in 1907; Ralph Adams Cram of Boston, who designed more than 100 churches in his career, took over and the building took on a more Gothic appearance rather than its Romanesque beginning.

Ground was broken for the nave May 8, 1916, by Bishop David H. Greer. It was virtually complete in less than 10 years. The west front was finished up to the bases of the towers, and the nave was completed for several years before it went into regular use. The altar and its timber canopy were placed at the east end of the nave in front of the old temporary wall of the crossing in 1939. The choir was then closed for remodeling.

In the fall of 1941, the temporary wall which separated the nave from the crossing was removed, and a service was held November 30 to celebrate the opening of the full length of the cathedral.

The third phase of construction began November 30, 1978, when cathedral trustees decided to finish the building.

Most visitors to St. John the Divine enter through the massive west front, which is 207 feet wide. The five portals are reflective of the five interior aisles. The bronze doors of the central portal were cast in Paris by Barbedienne, who also cast the Statue of Liberty. The 60 panels of those doors present scenes from the Bible executed by Henry Wilson. The stone carvings on the far left portal were done by John Angel of Boston and include St. Peter in the center and eight Christian martyrs. More carvings by Angel are found in the narthex above the doors, with representations of the Canterbury pilgrims and the Crusades.

The outside aisles of the enormous nave divide into 14 bays, each with a large window at the arcade level and a larger window at the clerestory level. The window in each bay depicts a particular field of human endeavor. For example, the first window on the north side is the sports bay and illustrates such subjects as boxing, bowling and auto racing. The windows in these bays are the works of several studios: Henry Willet, Charles J. Connick, Ernest W. Lakeman, Nicola D'Ascenzo, Wilbur H. Burnham and Reynolds-Francis-

Rohnstock. The rose window at the west end portrays spiritual gifts, the beatitudes and evangelists all radiating from Christ.

Three altars are in the nave: Lawyer's Bay on the north side with its walnut reredos carved by Pellegrini; Medical Bay, and All Souls' Bay, which contains a polychromed representation of paradise.

Two sets of tapestries, both dating from the 17th century, decorate various parts of the nave. One set is from weavers of Mortlake, England, and the other woven on papal looms founded by Cardinal Barberini in Rome. Both sets of tapestries depict scenes from the New Testament.

The eight round columns behind the altar, each 55 feet high and six feet in diameter, came from a quarry in Vinalhaven, Maine, and were set in place in 1904.

The pulpit is made of marble from Knoxville, Tennessee, and was designed by Henry Vaughan of Boston. The baptistry on the north side of the ambulatory contains a marble font dated 1928 which is the work of Albert H. Atkins of Boston.

Two large menorahs flank the high altar. They are bronze overlaid with gold and are designed after those used in the Temple of Jerusalem. Dedicated in 1930, they now serve as memorials to the Jews of the Holocaust.[3]

Behind the high altar, in the ambulatory, are seven chapels, each representing a distinct ethnic group. They were constructed between 1904 and 1918 and seat as many as 150. The chapels, from left to right, are: St. Ansgar, dedicated to Scandinavian people, featuring many figures in stone, including Martin Luther in the reredos; St. Boniface, dedicated to Germanic people, with windows by the Kempe Studio of England commemorating missionaries to all parts of the world; St. Columba, dedicated to people of English and Celtic origin, done in Romanesque style with grisaille-style windows by Burnham of Boston and others by Clayton and Bell of London. St. Martin's Chapel is of 13th century French Gothic design and honors French people, with a statue of St. Joan of Arc on the north wall, and beneath it a stone from the cell in Rouen from which she was led to the stake; St. Ambrose, dedicated to people of Italian descent, featuring Italian paintings and furniture and architecture of the Renaissance style; and St. James', honoring those of Spanish origin, which is the site of some services in Spanish.

The cathedral's organ was installed in 1910 by Ernest M. Skinner and rebuilt in 1954 by Aeolian-Skinner Co. It has 141 ranks and more than 8,000 pipes.

The 13-acre site on which the cathedral sits also contains Synod House, Diocesan House, Cathedral School and other buildings.

Cathedral of All Saints, Albany

Albany
East

Persons associated with Albany's magnificent cathedral have for years considered their building to be the first "great" cathedral of the Episcopal Church.

Others were established earlier, but Albany's building was the first to be built with the proportions of the great cathedrals of Europe. At 320 feet in length, it ranks fourth among American Episcopal cathedrals, topped only by those in New York, Washington and San Francisco.

The idea of a cathedral for New York's capital city came from William C. Doane, who was elected bishop after the Diocese of Albany was created from the Diocese of New York in 1868. St. Peter's Church, Albany, where Bishop Doane had been rector, offered its facilities for episcopal acts, but Bishop Doane accepted only with the proviso that it was a temporary arrangement.[4]

In his address to the first diocesan convention, in 1869, Bishop Doane said, "God helping me, if I live long enough, the Diocese of Albany will have the reality of a cathedral with all that involves of work and worship, in frequent services, in schools and houses of mercy of every kind."[5]

Bishop Doane's plan began with the formation of St. Agnes' School for Girls in 1870. A new congregation was formed in conjunction with the school by members of two other parishes, and property was donated for a cathedral building. At the end of that property was a disused machine shop of a foundry, which became the temporary site for worship on All Saints' Eve, October 31, 1872.

By 1875, a cathedral chapter was functioning, and a hospital begun, to be staffed in part by a new order of nuns formed by Bishop Doane, known as the Sisterhood of the Holy Child Jesus.[6]

Enough funds had been raised by 1882 to begin building.

The architectural plan of Robert W. Gibson, who proposed a building larger than the Episcopal Church previously had attempted, was accepted.[7]

The cornerstone was laid June 3, 1884, and by the fall of 1888, part of the Gothic revival building was ready for occupancy. It was dedicated November 20, 1888. The building of the choir, with triforium, clerestory, vaulted roof of stone and supported by flying buttresses, was finished in 1904. The roof of the nave, the lantern over the crossing and the towers at the west end of the building were unfinished.

Many lovely stained glass windows are found in the cathedral, including a rose window of the saints in glory over the entrance, executed by John LaFarge. The large window at the east end of the building is 64 feet high and in the upper portion commemorates various saints from the apostolic period to the Church of England. The window is from the studio of Clayton and Bell, London.

The Bishop's Eye rose window in the north transept is a reproduction of the famous one of the same name in Lincoln Cathedral and is from the Maitland Armstrong firm of New York City. Another large rose window by Clayton and Bell is found in the south transept. The six large windows in the nave are by Burleson and Grills of London and illustrate various angels and prophets. The cathedral's high altar is of polished pink granite on a block of Carlisle stone and was a gift from the sisterhood founded by Bishop Doane. The reredos contains a central panel of Christ reigning in glory with Mary and Joseph at the sides. Other furnishings of interest are the carved choir stalls, which came from a church in Bruges, Belgium, and are dated 1655, and the cathedra, made by Annesley and Company of Albany, which took one carver an entire year.[8]

Central New York

East

The spire of St. Paul's Cathedral is a landmark in Syracuse, soaring more than 200 feet high from its downtown site, and topped by a seven-foot cross.

The cathedral is the third building in Syracuse called St. Paul's. The first St. Paul's traces its organization to a small group which began to meet for worship in a Baptist church in 1824. The parish was formally organized in May, 1826, and soon a site was acquired for a building of its own.

A white clapboard building was constructed in 1827, and was consecrated September 18 of that year by John Henry Hobart, Bishop of New York. When William Barlow, first permanent clergyman for the parish, resigned in 1828, the congregation was unable to find a replacement, and the church was closed for more than two years, with occasional exceptions.[9]

During the 1830s, the congregation began to outgrow its little church, and the cornerstone for a new building was laid July 2, 1841. Construction took almost exactly a year, and the new edifice was consecrated July 5, 1842 by Bishop William H. DeLancey of Western New York. The new building was twice as large as its predecessor, built of native stone in late Gothic, or perpendicular, style.[10]

When the 1868 convention of the Diocese of Western New York voted to divide itself, the Diocese of Central New York was created. St. Paul's offered itself as a cathedral for the new diocese, but the offer was not accepted.

Bishop Frederick D. Huntington began to interest the diocese in the cathedral idea in 1882, although he had preached about it as early as 1869. At the same time, the federal government wanted to purchase the second St. Paul's for the site of a new post office.[11] The parish did sell its church to the government and began to make plans for a new building.

On May 21, 1883, the vestry of St. Paul's resolved to commit $70,000 to the building of a new cathedral. It also was decided that the edifice would be of gray limestone and designed by Henry Dudley of Brooklyn.[12]

The last service in the old building was on Christmas Day, 1883. The congregation then worshiped at St. James' Church until Whitsunday, 1884, when a chapel of the new building already was usable. On June 25, 1884, the cornerstone was laid for the new church. That church, which is the present cathedral, opened December 13, 1885.

Dudley's design was middle Gothic with pointed arches and windows common to English churches of the mid-13th to mid-14th centuries. The exterior was fashioned of Onandoga limestone, which came mostly from the reservation south of Syracuse, but also from the old St. Paul's.

St. Paul's first existence as a cathedral lasted only 12 years. Because of differences between Bishop Huntington and the rector and vestry of the parish, ties were broken and St. Paul's returned to parish status. It did not become a cathedral again until November, 1971, following an agreement between Bishop Ned Cole and the vestry.

Cracks were spotted in an arch to the chancel in 1984, and the building became unusable during the summer months. The congregation moved to the Church of the Saviour, the same church which had provided a temporary home exactly 100 years earlier when it was known as St. James.

The nave of St. Paul's can seat more than 900 and has a barrel roof constructed of stained pine.

The window above the high altar illustrates St. Paul preaching to the Athenians. The upper walls above the nave contain some brightly-colored clerestory windows. The interior walls of the building are made up of yellow and pink bricks.

Christ Church Cathedral, Hartford

Connecticut
East

Christ Church is one of the oldest buildings among Episcopal cathedrals, dating back to 1828, although it wasn't designated as a cathedral for another 90 years.

The parish also is one of the oldest, having been organized in 1762. By 1795, the congregation had its own building, which gradually became overcrowded. In 1826, the vestry appointed a committee to develop plans for a new church, and Ithiel Towne of New Haven was selected as architect.

The new building, which is the present cathedral, was erected in 1828, and was one of the first Gothic churches in the United States. It is a reflection of the enthusiasm of Nathaniel S. Wheaton, rector at the time, for the beauty of English cathedrals, especially York Minster.[13]

The bell tower was completed in 1833, and a Gothic cast-iron fence was added 20 years later. In 1879, the church was enlarged by the addition of the recessed chancel, and a parish building, which included a chapel.

A new look was given to the building in 1903, when the addition of buttresses and pinnacles was completed under the design of noted Hartford architect George Keller.

Early in the 20th century, discussions were being held about the establishment of a cathedral. The Diocese of Connecticut, formed in 1784, is the oldest in the Episcopal Church, but it did not have a cathedral. In 1913, the legislature granted a charter establishing the Cathedral Church of the Diocese of Connecticut. Bishop Chauncy B. Brewster established Christ Church as the cathedral June 15, 1919.

The cathedral is believed to be the oldest brownstone building in Hartford. Its interior is finished in dark oak. There are box pews with Roman numerals on the doors, a reminder of the period before 1881, when pews were rented.

The larger stained glass windows all were designed by the firm of Heaton, Butler and Bayne of London in the late 19th century. The three large windows in the south aisle depict Jesus meeting with Nathaniel, the Resurrection, and Christ on the road to Emmaus. The north aisle windows depict the Gloria in Excelsis, the Baptism of Jesus and the presentation of Christ to Simeon. Other windows of note are above the high altar, showing the Transfiguration, and above the baptismal font, portraying the three Marys at the tomb.

The high altar has carved front panels of the four gospel writers, and was inspired by the tomb of Archbishop Kemp in Canterbury Cathedral. The reredos, carved from Caen stone in 1919, shows 10 noted church leaders.

The Chapel of the Nativity, found at the head of the south aisle, was designed in 1907 by Ralph Adams Cram and contains some interesting appointments. The reredos above the altar contains four carved figures, including Samuel Seabury of Connecticut, the first American bishop, who holds a miniature of Christ Church.

One of the large brownstone panels in the entryway is engraved with a statement of the purpose of the cathedral made by Bishop Brewster in his 1912 diocesan convention address.[14]

In 1989, the cathedral embarked on a renovation plan. The first phase, which involved masonry work and exterior improvements, focusing on the walls and roof, was finished in 1990, but after spending $1.1 million for the refurbishing, there was no more money for interior work. Then James W. Bain, a 61-year-old retired supervisor for a utility, took over, washing and scraping walls, fixing damaged plaster, and painting walls and ceilings. Mr. Bain said his work is being done as a memorial to his son, Douglas, a former cathedral choirboy who died of cancer at age 15.[15]

Long Island
East

Long Island's beautiful cathedral was made possible by a single donor, and stands as a memorial to Alexander T. Stewart from his wife, Cornelia.

Stewart bought more than 7,000 acres of the Hempstead Plains of Long Island in 1869 and had plans for the development of the property, including a model village. Stewart's concept included a church for the village, but he died suddenly in 1876, before completion of his plan.[16]

Cornelia Stewart made a free offering to the Diocese of Long Island for a church, schools and the bishop's house, as long as those buildings would become the seat of the Bishop of Long Island, and that the crypt in the cathedral be the resting place of her husband.[17]

Henry G. Harrison of New York City was chosen as architect for the cathedral. The cornerstone, dated 1876, was laid June 28, 1877 by Abram N. Littlejohn, first Bishop of Long Island. Harrison's original plan was reduced substantially by executors of the Stewart estate.

The first service in the new cathedral was April 12, 1885. It was consecrated June 2, 1885, by Bishop Littlejohn. The building is of floriated 13th century Gothic architecture. It is cruciform in shape with a spire, baptistry, organ chamber, apse, chancel, chantry and crypt. The exterior is made of Belleville, New Jersey, stone and the interior of Berea, Ohio, stone. Several kinds of marble are found in the interior. Unlike most Gothic cathedrals, Harrison positioned carved bosses that resembled heads of European rulers, rather than the more typical gargoyles.[18]

The cathedral underwent major renovation inside and out, from 1948-50, and other refurbishings took place between 1964 and 1970.

There are some impressive examples of stained glass windows, designed and executed by the English firm of Clayton and Bell. The windows in the nave and choir illustrate the story of the Incarnation. One of the most interesting windows is the large one in the south transept known as the Te Deum window. It symbolizes the Incarnation, Atonement, the glory of the Lord and the adoration of the Lamb. The Jesse window dominates the north transept.

The apse contains 13 lancet windows, with Christ the Good Shepherd in the center and six of his apostles on each side.

The free-standing high altar was made of marble in Antwerp, Belgium, and contains carved panels of the Annunciation, adoration of the Magi, the Crucifixion, the Resurrection and the supper at Emmaus. The credence table also has some fine examples of stone carving.

Other interesting features of the cathedral are the fan vaulting over the nave, and the altar in the south transept, which was erected in 1950 as a memorial to men and women of the cathedral who served in World Wars I and II.

The Chapel of the Resurrection, at the east end of the undercroft, was redesigned and refurbished in 1964-65, and features a finely-ribbed, fan-vaulted rotunda. A free-standing altar of white Vermont marble stands in the midst of the rotunda. Behind the altar stands the processional cross of the Bishop of Long Island, which was fashioned in England. The windows surrounding the rotunda were designed and made in England by the firm of Heaton, Butler and Bayne.

The cathedral's organ, rebuilt in 1962-63 by the Schlicker Organ Company of Buffalo, includes the main instrument in the chancel and another in the tower. The tower contains 13 bells which were cast in Philadelphia in 1876 for the United States Centennial Exhibition and represent the 13 colonies. They have been in use at the cathedral since 1883.

Maine
East

One of the earliest buildings being constructed as a cathedral was in the Diocese of Maine, where planning was begun in 1867.

St. Luke's parish was founded in 1851, when the need arose for a second Episcopal church in Portland. Bishop Horatio Southgate, a native of Portland and missionary bishop in Constantinople, returned to Maine, met with a group of about 20 persons and held the first service April 27, 1851, in a union hall.

The congregation soon needed a building of its own and secured a lot in 1854. Construction began in that year, and the first service in the new building was held June 30, 1855.

In the fall of 1866, the Diocese of Maine couldn't afford to pay the salary of its bishop, so in order to provide him with a living, the bishop was made rector of a parish.[19] In January, 1867, newly-elected Bishop Henry A. Neely became the rector of St. Luke's, and plans were soon made for the building of a cathedral.

St. Luke's sold its building to another congregation, and architect Charles C. Haight of New York City was selected to design the new cathedral. The cornerstone was laid by Bishop Neely August 15, 1867. The building was generally in English Gothic design of a rectangular shape. Stone from a quarry in Cape Elizabeth, Maine, was used for the exterior, with some finishing free stone from Nova Scotia. The interior walls were plastered, and the peaked roof of wood was supported by wooden beams and trusses of black ash.

The first service in the new church was held on Christmas Day, 1868, even through the building wasn't complete. A service of consecration was held on the Feast of St. Luke, October 18, 1877.

Construction began on a parish house in 1892, and that building, which provides space for offices, classrooms and meetings, was finished in 1894.

The next building project was the construction of Emmanuel Chapel, which was completed in 1905. The chapel, used for daily services, is renowned for its architecture. An outstanding work of ecclesiastical art is the altarpiece, "The American Madonna," painted by John Lafarge for the chapel.

In 1925, the high altar, made of French marble, was installed with the intricately-carved oak reredos. The main subject of the reredos is the Incarnation, with a statue of the Virgin Mary the dominant figure in the center.

The original plans for the cathedral included an entrance tower, but when funds were not available, the tower was not constructed. A temporary wooden porch served for 91 years until a bequest in 1957 provided for the construction of a tower with bell.[20] The project was completed in 1958, and includes a bell weighing 2,350 pounds which was cast in England.

In 1964-65, the parish house was renovated and enlarged.

St. Luke's contains many beautiful stained glass windows. The windows in the nave are biblical scenes and were executed in 1879. The rose window above the reredos depicts the Ascension and was installed in 1900. Because of deterioration, that window needed emergency repairs in 1991 and had to be removed. It was shipped to a New York firm, then returned to the stonework, which was repaired and waterproofed.[21]

The two lancet windows on the sides of the reredos also were installed in 1879, and depict the Crucifixion and the Resurrection. Other windows of note include the four seen in the tower as one enters the cathedral, which represent the four evangelists.

The Cathedral Church of St. Paul is unusual among American cathedrals in that it is the only example of Greek revival architecture.

The present building dates to 1819, and served as a parish church for nearly 100 years before being dedicated as a cathedral.

St. Paul's was founded when a group of Boston patriots wanted to establish the first entirely American Episcopal parish. A group met in 1818 for this purpose, aware that two other Boston parishes—Christ Church (Old North Church) and Trinity—already existed, but they had originated with the pre-Revolutionary War Church of England.[22]

Alexander Parris and Solomon Williard were commissioned in 1819 by the founders to design and construct a building of Greek revival style to contrast with Boston's existing colonial and Gothic structures.[23]

The new building was completed in 1820. The body is of light Quincy granite and the Ionic columns on the portico are of brown sandstone from Stafford County, Virginia. Stones from St. Paul's Cathedral, London; St. Botolph's, Boston, England; and Valley Forge were incorporated into the building. The new church was consecrated June 30, 1820, by Bishop Alexander Griswold of Massachusetts.

The church was completely redecorated about 1875. A large stained glass window showing St. Paul preaching to the Athenians was installed in the wall behind the altar. Paintings of two evangelists were done on both sides of the window.

More improvements were made in 1891. The organ was removed from the gallery and a new one was installed in the chancel, along with stalls for a choir of men and boys. In addition, the chancel floor was carried forward six feet into the church.

In 1904, two sisters, Misses Mary Sophia and Harriet Sarah Walker of Waltham, left an estate of more than a million dollars "for the purpose of building, establishing and maintaining a cathedral, or bishop's church, of the Protestant Episcopal Church in the city of Boston."[24]

The diocese accepted the bequest in 1906, and Bishop William Lawrence decided that an existing church should be designated as a cathedral. St. Paul's location seemed ideal, and on October 7, 1912, the downtown church began its new life as a cathedral.

In 1927, the architectural firm of Cram and Ferguson redesigned the interior and accomplished the following: The chancel was deepened and the choir stalls were placed within the chancel walls, the chancel floor was repaved in black and white marble, two windows were placed in the curved wall behind the altar, and a reredos of American walnut was installed behind a new altar made of Algerian onyx. A new pulpit and sounding board, communion rail, lectern and deacons bench, all designed by Ralph Adams Cram, were installed.

In 1932, Dean Philemon F. Sturges announced, in accordance with the idea that the cathedral was the church of all people, that St. Paul's would not accept transfers from any parish church. Three years later, he declared, "Here at St. Paul's we are trying to reduce the number of communicants and to discourage attendance at Sunday School."[25] To further that idea, most parish organizations were dissolved in the 1940s.

Additional renovations were made in 1952 and 1962. In the first improvements, the windows in the curve behind the altar were removed, a new organ was placed in the west gallery, choir stalls were removed and the chancel repaved.

Trinity Cathedral, Trenton

New Jersey
East

The idea of a cathedral for the Diocese of New Jersey was discussed as early as the 1850s, but it was another 100 years before that notion became a reality.

The present cathedral grew out of a merger of two Trenton parishes, Trinity and All Saints'. Trinity was formed first, in 1858 when a group of 39 former members of St. Michael's Church, the first established in Trenton, met to discuss a new congregation.

Construction began soon afterward, and a new building was completed in 1860. Trinity was plagued by financial problems for many years, and finally was able to overcome its debts just after the turn of the century.

Meanwhile, another parish was being established in the western part of Trenton. A small group began to meet for Evening Prayer in 1894 and by 1896 had progressed to the point where a cornerstone could be laid for a new church. That building was dedicated in 1897 and was known as All Saints' Church. It was replaced by a new building in 1927.

The cathedral idea was considered again during the 1920s, and in 1930, the Diocesan Convention, led by Bishop Paul Matthews, called for the establishment of a cathedral in Trenton. In that same year, it was determined that Trinity Parish did not have enough land for the proposed cathedral, so a plan was formed in which All Saints would invite Trinity to merge and become Trinity Cathedral Parish. The merger was accomplished, and land adjacent to All Saints' was acquired.

Construction began in 1935 with the building of the Norman-style crypt. The first service in the crypt was held January 5, 1936, and the congregation worshiped there for the next 18 years.

In November, 1952, construction began on the superstructure of the cathedral. The first service in the new Gothic building was held January 24, 1954.

An education building was constructed in 1960 as a home for the Cathedral Day School and the Sunday school. Also added were St. Helier's Chapel in the north transept of the cathedral, and a memorial garden. Trinity was consecrated by Bishop Alfred L. Banyard September 26, 1965.

The original All Saints' Church became Synod Hall, and the second All Saints' is now known as All Saints' Chapel.

As one enters the west door of the cathedral, there are limestone statues on both sides of the entrance: an angel of the Resurrection and St. Michael the Archangel.

At the other end of the building, the high altar is made of Italian marble and is the one which was used at old Trinity Church. The reredos is of limestone and has carvings of Moses on the right side and St. John the Evangelist at the left.

St. Elizabeth's Chapel is in the south transept and has a white marble altar, and, above the credence table, a carved wooden representation of the Last Supper brought from Oberammergau. Above the altar are some fine Russian icons from the 17th and 18th centuries. One came from a czar's private chapel, and the other hung in a Moscow cathedral.

Nearby is a statue of the Virgin Mother and Child carved in the 15th century French mode. It was polychromed by Valentine D'Ogres, the artist who executed the stained glass windows and polychromed the stations of the cross, which hang on the side walls of the nave.

Among the cathedral's interesting windows are those on the right side of the nave which depict Jesus and John the Baptist as children, and St. Augustine with a Bible.

Newark

East

Trinity-St. Philip's Cathedral, a building with a distinct colonial style of architecture, had its beginnings in the early part of the 18th century.

There were services for colonists who had settled in Newark as early as 1729, conducted by visiting priests. In 1742, Newark's Anglicans had organized and decided to construct their own building. A small stone edifice with a steeple was erected on almost the same site as the present cathedral and completed in 1743. Five years later, King George II granted a charter to Trinity.

During the Revolutionary War, the church was used as a hospital by both British and American troops. Later, American forces used the building as a gymnasium.[26] The church was badly damaged by the soldiers and received even more harm following the war when a mob raided the building in 1778, smashing windows and doors, cutting holes in the roof, and stealing hangings from the pulpit (Anglicanism was often a target of patriot mobs because of its relationship to the British crown).[27]

Trinity was allotted a sum of money by the American Congress to help pay for the damages, but the destruction was so extensive that plans were made for a new church.

The old building was torn down, but the tower left intact to be used in the construction of the new church. A building fund was organized, with income derived by the sale of pews and subscriptions. Construction began in 1809, and the colonial-style building, which is the present cathedral, was completed the following year.

During the 1800s, Trinity not only experienced steady growth itself; it also became involved in the establishment of 10 other Episcopal churches.[28]

In 1857, the church building was enlarged at the east end by adding a chancel and sanctuary, giving Trinity basically the same appearance it has today.

Until 1874, Trinity had been part of the Diocese of New Jersey. But on November 12 of that year, the diocese was divided in two, and Trinity became part of the Diocese of Northern New Jersey. It was renamed the Diocese of Newark in 1886.

When Trinity observed its 150th anniversary in 1896, new furniture was added, including a lectern and pulpit.

The question of whether to have a cathedral in the Diocese of Newark was discussed in 1906. A year later, Christ Church, Newark, was designated pro-cathedral for the young diocese. That designation lasted only 10 years, for in 1917 Trinity became the pro-cathedral.[29] The cathedral idea was developed further in 1931, when 38 acres were purchased as a site for a building to be known as the Cathedral of All Saints.[30] Because of the Great Depression and World War II, the idea of a cathedral in that location was abandoned.

Trinity achieved full cathedral status in May, 1944, when it merged with the Cathedral Chapter of All Saints.

A parish house was built in 1910, and it was replaced in 1944 by a larger Cathedral House. Extensive renovation took place in the late 1940s and forced the cathedral to be closed for a lengthy period.[31]

Another merger took place in 1966. When fire destroyed St. Philip's Church, that congregation, once a mission of Trinity, had no place to worship. On May 21 of that year, the predominantly black St. Philip's and the largely white Trinity merged. The following year, Dillard Robinson was elected dean, the first black dean of a cathedral in the United States.[32] St. Philip's name was added to Trinity's in 1992.

Rhode Island

East

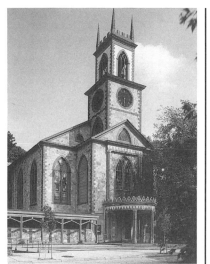

Based on the date of the founding of the parish, St. John's would be the oldest Episcopal cathedral in the United States.

The Cathedral of St. John can trace its roots back to 1722, when on June 11, the Feast of St. Barnabas, the cornerstone for King's Church was laid. Lots had been purchased by a small group of Anglicans, and a modest wooden building was erected. At that time, of course, there was no Episcopal Church or United States of America, so Anglicans in Providence turned to the Society for the Propagation of the Gospel in Foreign Parts in an attempt to find clergy.

The society sent George Pigot, and the congregation had its first in a long line of clergy. The congregation experienced modest growth, and the building had a tower and steeple added. When the Revolutionary War broke out, the church was closed for nine years.

In 1790, the Diocese of Rhode Island was formed, and four years later a new charter was issued to the church by the state with the new name of St. John's.

Age and hurricanes weakened the church building, and in 1810 it was demolished in order that a new edifice could be built. John Holden Greene, who designed other Providence buildings, was chosen as the architect. He selected a Georgian design with Gothic trim, Gothic detail and a Gothic tower. The cornerstone was laid November 5, 1810, and on June 11, 1811, again the Feast of St. Barnabas, the building which is the present cathedral, was consecrated by Bishop Alexander V. Griswold.

The church was enlarged in 1868. The eastern wall was removed and transepts and a shallow chancel were added. When the south transept was being constructed, a stone which had been part of the foundation of the original King's Church was inserted into the outer wall.[33]

Another expansion took place in 1905, when a choir and sanctuary were added, making the church cruciform in plan. A new chancel screen and the sanctuary gave St. John's a look reminiscent of the period when the original King's Church was built, rather than Victorian Gothic.[34]

A year later, discussions began to take place about the possibility of St. John's becoming a cathedral. Bishop William M. McVickar mentioned the idea publicly, but it wasn't until 1929, under Bishop James Perry, when St. John's achieved cathedral status.

A major renovation of the cathedral took place in 1967. A circular altar rail was installed at the crossing, pews were replaced by chairs, the pulpit was moved forward to take advantage of the acoustics of the dome, and there were general restorations both outside and inside.

A relic of the 1722 church is set in the wall above the entrance. It is a piece of wood painted black with a text in gold and was part of the sanctuary of the old church.

The baptistry also contains historic furnishings. The "William and Mary" chair dates to the 17th century, the font was part of the furnishings from the old church, and the wooden cross on the wall was made from a timber in the Old Narragansett Glebe House.

The 62-foot dome above the crossing has interesting plaster decoration. The Waterford glass chandelier was given to St. John's in 1816. The altar is an open ball claw table from the 18th century and was used in the Old Narragansett Church.

Among the windows are three in the sanctuary crafted by the E.C. Kempe Company of London, representing Christ the King, over the altar; the calling of Matthew, in the south transept; and Christ blessing the children, in the north transept.

Vermont
East

Vermont's striking cathedral is among the newest in the Episcopal Church, having been consecrated in 1973. The contemporary building is situated in an urban renewal area of downtown Burlington, and is the successor to an earlier St. Paul's, which was destroyed by fire.

St. Paul's was organized in 1830, three years before the Diocese of Vermont was formed. At the 1833 convention of the new diocese, Bishop John Henry Hopkins noted that his "first Episcopal act was the consecration of the new church at Burlington, by the name of St. Paul's, on the 25th of November."[35]

Bishop Hopkins had been elected Bishop of Vermont with the understanding that he also would be the rector of St. Paul's, an arrangement which lasted 26 years.

The first Gothic church was enlarged in 1851 and again in 1866. A chapel and parish house were added in 1882, and another enlargement was made in 1904. In 1910, a serious fire occurred, but it was contained to the area where the parish house joined the church before major damage occurred in either building.

The church was redecorated in 1952, and another renovation and expansion was made in 1962-64. A new educational wing was built, and extensive work was done on the parish house.

In 1966, St. Paul's was made the cathedral by vote of diocesan convention. Although St. Paul's Church never had been formally made the cathedral, since Bishop Hopkins had established his throne in its chancel it had served many of the purposes of a cathedral church, and each successive bishop, particularly Bishop Arthur Hall, took active interest in the work of St. Paul's Parish.[36]

A fire of unknown origin, which burned for many hours, destroyed St. Paul's 140-year-old building and complex on February 15, 1971.

The decision was made to rebuild, and the new cathedral was finished two years later. The parish sold the site of the old building to the renewal developer of downtown Burlington. In exchange, the parish received $300,000 and another piece of property, which doubled the cathedral's land holdings downtown.

The firm Burlington Associates was chosen to design the new cathedral following an architectural competition. Meanwhile, the congregation worshiped in a bank lobby, a vacant office, the educational wing of the destroyed building, a Roman Catholic chapel, and an Episcopal chapel which serves the University of Vermont.[37]

Construction began during the summer of 1972, and the new cathedral, a contemporary structure of poured concrete, steel and glass, was dedicated November 11, 1973, by Bishop Harvey Butterfield, 999 days after the fire.

In the proposal for the new cathedral, the following vision was described: "The vision of St. Paul's is not to reconstruct the former program, but rather that of a new city cathedral, a living church of the 20th and 21st centuries."[38]

As one enters the cathedral through the south lobby, an icon of St. Paul is seen. The icon, executed by Ivan Dicke, symbolizes the bond with the Eastern Church. Inside, a large cross hangs on the wall, fashioned from metal, spikes and hand-wrought nails salvaged from the remnants of the old church.

The altar, pulpit, lectern, cathedra and other furnishings in the sanctuary were designed and built by the Wippell Mowbray Studios of Exeter, England. A chapel is located behind the sanctuary.

Christ Church Cathedral, Springfield

Western Massachusetts
East

The U.S. military had a prominent role in the early days of Christ Church, one of the oldest of the nation's cathedral congregations. It served as a parish church for more than 100 years before receiving cathedral status.

The congregation can trace its roots to 1817, when Col. Roswell Lee, commander of the Army in Springfield, established the "Chapel on Armory Hill." On May 24, 1821, the first resident priest, Edwin Rutledge, organized the parish and it was named Christ Church.[39]

Three years later, on March 2, 1824, a fire forced the Army to use the chapel for factory purposes. The congregation, then served by visiting clergymen, held its services in a nearby Methodist church.

From 1838-40, services were held in the Town Hall while a church was being built. The congregation's first building of its own was completed in April, 1840, and consecrated by Bishop Alexander V. Griswold of Massachusetts.[40]

The need for a larger church became evident in the 1870s. The architectural firm of Lord, Fuller and Wadlin of Boston was contracted to design the new building. The cornerstone was laid November 10, 1875, and the first service in what is now the cathedral was held May 21, 1876. The structure is of Norman architecture constructed of Longmeadow brownstone.

Not long after occupancy of the new building, a problem occurred in the tower. Cracks were found which made the tower appear unsafe, so it was removed. It was rebuilt in 1927.[41]

Christ Church remained part of the Diocese of Massachusetts until 1901, when the Diocese of Western Massachusetts was created. Although there were suggestions as early as 1919 that Christ Church be made the cathedral of the new diocese, it didn't become a reality until 1929.[42]

Upon entering the cathedral, a visitor sees narthex windows containing seals from Christ Church Cathedrals all over the Anglican Communion.

Moving inside, the focus is on the high altar and its reredos. The altar is of Italian white Botticino marble and, like most of the other appointments, was added in the 20th century. The wooden reredos has a central panel depicting the Ascension. On each side are carved large figures of the four evangelists. The carvings and other woodwork in the cathedral, were done by Alois Lang, of the well-known wood-carving family from Oberammergau.

The lectern is a hand-carved wood piece originally designed for Washington Cathedral. The lectern had been too small for the Washington building and was moved to Springfield in 1957.

There are many examples of fine stained glass in the cathedral, including rose windows above the entrance and in both transepts. The rose windows are 19th century antique glass and were made by Otto Falch & Co. of Boston. All the windows were releaded and restored in 1973. The chancel windows are of English glass made by Heaton, Butler and Bayne of London, and depict scenes from the life of Jesus. The clerestory windows were made by C.E. Kempe & Co. of London, and also are scenes from the life of Jesus.

In December, 1991, a major restoration was completed. The project included interior plastering and painting, relocation of the altar from the reredos to a freestanding position, repositioning of the organ, and new lighting and sound systems.

Western New York

East

St. Paul's is one of the earliest cathedrals of the Episcopal Church, having been so designated in 1866.

It also is one of the oldest congregations among cathedrals. The certificate of incorporation of St. Paul's is February 10, 1817. Two years later, land was donated for a church building and the cornerstone laid. In 1821, the original frame church was consecrated, making St. Paul's the first permanent church building in what was then the village of Buffalo. An unusual ecumenical event for its time took place that year when a Roman Catholic priest from Rochester celebrated Mass in St. Paul's for the few members of his faith who lived in Buffalo.

That first church was sold in 1850 to a German evangelical congregation, and construction soon began on the present cathedral. Richard Upjohn, a notable church architect, was chosen to design the new building. William DeLancey, the first Bishop of Western New York, laid the cornerstone that year. The Victorian Gothic stone church was completed the following year and consecrated by Bishop DeLancey. Two years later, the first set of bells was placed in the tower.

In 1866, the vestry of St. Paul's offered the church as the cathedral for the diocese, and the offer was accepted by Bishop Arthur C. Cox.

A major renovation took place in 1953, with the exterior stonework being repointed and the interior undergoing re-conditioning and repainting. The chancel area was extended and the choir seating area enlarged in 1960.

St. Paul's celebrated its 150th anniversary in 1967 with special events throughout the year. The columbarium in the lower level of the cathedral was dedicated that year, and the tabernacle was installed in the chapel.

Additional renovation took place in 1979-80, when the interior was replastered and repainted and the exterior stone work repointed. Preservation cleaning of the exterior was completed in 1985.

The cathedral's spire is a landmark in downtown Buffalo, rising 274 feet above street level. It contains a ring of 14 bells, which are played by hand several times a day.

Two interesting pieces of stone donated by Bishop Charles Brent may be found in the cathedral. A fragment of a pillar from Cloth Hall in Ypres, Belgium, is mounted in the narthex. Bishop Brent had been chief of chaplains for the American forces in World War I before becoming Bishop of Western New York in 1918. The other item donated by Bishop Brent is a fragment of the high altar of Notre Dame Cathedral, Rheims, on the south wall of the sanctuary.

Another stone of note is located near the Bishop's stall on the left side of the chancel. It is a fragment of the wall of Canterbury Cathedral dating back to 1098-1100, and was donated in 1926 by the dean of Canterbury.

St. Paul's contains some beautiful stained glass windows. The window above the high altar is of the Ascension. Nearby, on the north side of the chancel, the windows illustrate the Eucharist and the Resurrection, and on the south side of the chancel, the Palm Sunday procession, Christ before Pilate, and the Crucifixion. The windows on the south side of the nave portray scenes from the life of Christ, with the upper section of each window showing a parallel event in the Old Testament.

Southwest

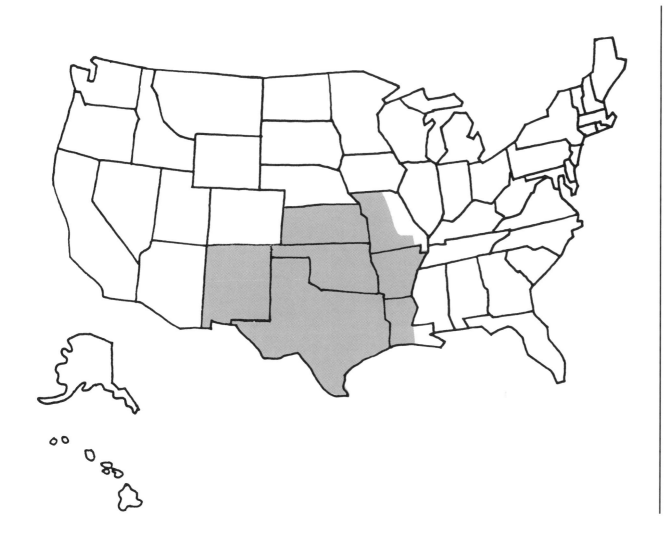

The Dioceses of

Western Kansas
Arkansas
Dallas
Kansas
Oklahoma
Rio Grande
Texas
West Missouri
Western Louisiana

Christ Cathedral, Salina

Western Kansas
Southwest

It may seem a bit unusual to find a handsome Gothic cathedral in the middle of Kansas, but such a building does in fact exist.

Occasional Episcopal services were held in Salina as early as 1868, but it was 1870 before a parish was organized. Christ Church was organized April 12 of that year and the congregation had a small, frame church erected by 1872, and consecrated in 1874.

In 1901, the Diocese of Kansas was divided, with the western two-thirds of the state to be administered as a missionary district by General Convention. Sheldon M. Griswold of Hudson, New York, was consecrated bishop for the new missionary district on January 8, 1903. He took up residence in his see city of Salina in 1903 and began to talk about the possibility of a cathedral almost at once.

The Christ Church vestry offered Bishop Griswold use of the church as a pro-cathedral, but the bishop's idea was a cathedral of the English pattern. A cathedral chapter was organized June 30, 1903, and a constitution and bylaws were adopted the following month.

A prominent person in the founding of Christ Cathedral is Mrs. Sarah Elizabeth Batterson, widow of a priest, who resided in Hudson, New York. Bishop Griswold found Mrs. Batterson was eager to erect a cathedral in the West as a memorial to her husband, who had been a missionary priest in Texas, Minnesota and the Dakotas, and later a rector in Philadelphia.

The entire cathedral is the gift of Mrs. Batterson, and includes communion vessels which were made from her jewelry following her death.[1]

Henry A. Macomb and Charles M. Burns of Philadelphia were engaged as architects, and ground was broken for the cathedral on April 2, 1906, by Bishop Griswold. The cornerstone was laid May 29 the same year. Nearly one year later, the last stone was laid to complete the tower.

The first service in the new building was January 8, 1908, the fifth anniversary of Bishop Griswold's consecration. The cathedral was consecrated May 28, 1908, Ascension Day.

Christ Cathedral is of early English Gothic style, with construction of native Kansas stone. It has a massive central bell tower containing a chime of 11 bells, each of which is inscribed with a verse from Psalm 150. Three additional bells were given in 1989. The building is composed of a nave, transepts and choir with four great arches supporting the central tower over the crossing.

Persons who enter the cathedral through the narthex find windows and doors formed by 10 arches. Within each arch is a leaded, stained glass window portraying one of the beatitudes.

All the woodwork is in black oak. The carving was done by members of the Lang family of Oberammergau. A striking appointment is the rood beam with hand-carved figures.

The high altar is of Carthage marble and has an imposing reredos of Silverdale stone. The lectern, pulpit and altar rail are memorials to the first three bishops of Kansas.

The Chapel of St. Mary, dedicated in 1911, has an altar, altar rail and lectern which originally were in old Christ Church. Blessed Sacrament Chapel was paid for by offerings of Sunday school students over several years. In 1982, a columbarium was installed on the east wall of the chapel and the chapel was redesigned.

There are fine examples of stained glass windows in the cathedral. The five windows behind the reredos of the high altar depict Christ the King in the center, flanked by the four angels named in scripture: Uriel, Michael, Gabriel and Raphael.

The large window in the south transept is of English glass and depicts the Last Supper.

The General Convention of 1970 created the Diocese of Western Kansas and William Davidson, who had been bishop of the missionary district, was elected as the first bishop of Western Kansas.

The cathedral's organ was built by the M.P. Moller Company of Hagerstown, Maryland, and is a three-manual instrument of 43 ranks. It was dedicated in 1977.

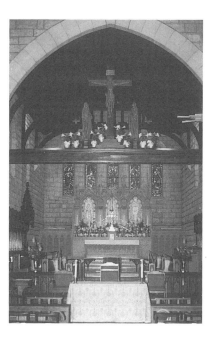

Arkansas
Southwest

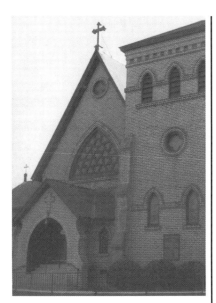

The building of Trinity Cathedral is due largely to the work of one man—The Rt. Rev. Henry N. Pierce.

Bishop Pierce came to Little Rock in 1870 as Missionary Bishop of Arkansas and the Indian Territory. After his arrival, he felt the diocese should have a cathedral. He discussed that possibility with the vestry of Christ Church, but that congregation declined his offer, so Bishop Pierce decided to build a cathedral.

After the diocese approved the idea of a cathedral in 1879, Bishop Pierce visited the East to raise funds for the project. There was little money available in Arkansas in the years following the Civil War, so he turned elsewhere.

In 1882, three lots were purchased, and because funds were limited, it was decided to build the cathedral in three stages. Ground was broken in January, 1884, and the nave was completed late that year. The first service in the new building was October 19, 1884, Bishop Pierce's 64th birthday. Following completion of the first stage, the east end of the building was boarded up and the altar located at the west end.

The second stage of construction took place in 1889 and added transepts and the crossing. The altar then was moved to the north transept, and the east end of the transepts and the crossing were closed off.

The third stage, the chancel, was completed in time for Easter Day, 1892, and the brick building was complete. The altar was moved to its current location at the east end of the building.

Bishop Pierce's son, the Rev. A.W. Pierce, had studied architecture, and drew the plans for the cathedral. The cruciform-shaped building is a rural adaptation of English Gothic design with hints of Romanesque. All elements of Gothic style are included, even though they aren't developed as they are in larger churches. For example, the clerestory elevation was built, despite the fact that it isn't high enough for windows, so dormers were placed above to provide light.

The chapel was built in 1924, on the site which had been used as a choir room. Trinity's original altar and reredos were placed in the chapel, a memorial to Bishop Pierce. The chapel was remodeled in 1958, and again in 1981.

One of the oldest parts of the cathedral is the baptistry, which was a portion of the first stage. The baptistry, with its domed ceiling and miniature trefoil decoration, appears just as it did in 1884, with the exception of the font, which was given by Sunday school students in 1901, and the windows, which were added in 1956.

The high altar and reredos were given in 1924. A figure of Christ, carved in Oberammergau by Anton Lang, dominates the reredos. The other two figures, of St. John and St. Mary, also were carved in Oberammergau and were installed in 1961.

The pulpit was given in 1905 and the lectern in 1918. The small pews in the chancel and south transept area are from the cathedral's original chapel. Most of the other furnishings in the chancel date from the 1950s.

Another major memorial to Bishop Pierce is the east window over the high altar. It was given in 1909, and portrays the church universal, the church militant, the church spiritual and the church triumphant, with a large figure of Christ at the center.

The window in the north transept illustrates the Benedicite canticle, and was designed by an Englishman named Beadel in the early 1950s. His signature in the window is a beetle. The south transept window was installed in 1939 and depicts "Suffer the little children to come unto me" (Mark 10:14).

Dallas
Southwest

St. Matthew's was one of the first cathedrals established west of the Mississippi River, but none of its present buildings dates before 1910.

St. Matthew's was founded in May, 1857, by the Rev. George Rottenstein, and was the first Episcopal parish organized in North Texas. Rottenstein conducted a service as early as May 25, 1856, in an old storehouse on Main Street, which is now the site of El Centro Community College, and in a Masonic Lodge in the area now part of the West End.

In 1870, the Rev. Silas Davenport arrived in Dallas to serve the young congregation and work soon began on the first of four buildings St. Matthew's would occupy.

The church was designated the cathedral of the Missionary District of Northern Texas by Bishop Alexander C. Garrett in 1875. Davenport became the first dean and was responsible for a second St. Matthew's being constructed and occupied in June, 1877. The brick structure was called "the most handsome church in town" by a Dallas newspaper, and the bell from the first church was moved to the new building.

In 1895, the same year that the Diocese of Dallas was organized, the third building was completed, and it remained the center of diocesan life until 1929. The diocese has been divided twice, with the Diocese of North Texas being organized in 1910, and the Diocese of Fort Worth in 1982.

The cathedral moved to its present location in 1929. Formerly a downtown church, St. Matthew's was able to move to the 10-acre site of St. Mary's College when that school closed after 30 years of operation. An agreement was reached with the bishop and diocese, and the cathedral assumed the indebtedness of St. Mary's, amortizing it within a relatively short period of time.

The present cathedral is an enlargement of the St. Mary's College chapel. Refurbishment and renovation have made St. Matthew's a spacious representation of the neo-Gothic building movement so common in America in the 19th century. Architect George Dahl designed the lengthening and widening of the chapel to accommodate the cathedral congregation.[2] This was intended to be a temporary measure until funds could be raised for the building of a grand new cathedral. Because of the Great Depression of the 1930s and World War II, that plan was never brought to fruition.

In the early 1970s, the cathedral chapter decided to put aside the idea for a great cathedral building and to concentrate instead on the establishment of a long-term program of establishing new ministries.

The cathedral's bell, known as Great Matthew, was installed in 1945 after having been rung in St. Matthew's earlier buildings. It was rescued from a salvage yard by a parishioner.[3] It stands in front of the Great Hall.

St. Matthew's is in possession of some Tiffany windows, which were never installed in the current building. When the move was made to the current cathedral, none of the Tiffanys could fit, so they were dismantled, catalogued and put into storage in the cathedral basement, where they remain in poor condition.[4]

Original art glass windows are found over the high altar. Because the building was originally the chapel for a girls' school, women are depicted—the Nativity in the center flanked by St. Agnes and St. Ursula. The windows on each side of that center window are of the Annunciation and Jesus with Mary and Martha.

Several appointments from the previous cathedral are found in the chancel, including the cathedra, pulpit, lectern and brass chancel rail.

Grace Cathedral, Topeka

Kansas
Southwest

Like many cathedrals, Grace Cathedral, Topeka, is unfinished. But this one continues to build to restore a building nearly destroyed by fire.

The congregation's history dates to January 20, 1857, when the Rev. Charles M. Calloway, who came to Topeka from Maryland under the sponsorship of the Episcopal Missionary Association, held the first service. There was so much interest in the formation of an Episcopal church in Topeka that on the day after that first service, two lots were offered to Calloway for a church and rectory if he would continue to hold services.

Calloway did remain and held services in Topeka's Constitution Hall for the congregation which called itself Grace Mission.

Later in 1857, Calloway went east and raised funds for "The Episcopal Female Seminary at Tecumseh," and in 1859, ground was broken for that girls' school.

In 1860, a group of city founders offered Calloway 20 acres if he would abandon the Tecumseh site and establish the school in Topeka. He left Tecumseh with only the foundation laid, and began the school in Topeka.

Services were moved to the girls school in 1861 and construction began on a church building. The congregation moved to its new building during the summer of 1865.

In 1877 Thomas Vail, Bishop of Kansas, began to speak of the possibility of Grace Church becoming the cathedral. At the convention of the Diocese of Kansas in 1879, Grace offered itself as the cathedral, and it became the bishop's church on June 5, 1879.

Plans were soon made for a new cathedral building, which would be located on the property of the College of the Sisters of Bethany (Calloway's girls' school). The cornerstone for a guild hall was laid in September, 1888, with the intention that the guild hall would be used for services until the cathedral was finished. Because of poor economic conditions, the guild hall was built at a large debt, and plans to build the cathedral were put aside.

A large gift early in the 20th century rekindled the idea of a cathedral, and ground was broken for the present building in 1909. Work proceeded rapidly, and the Kansas Silverdale limestone exterior was completed in 1912, but funds ran out again and the building stood empty until 1916. A capital funds campaign that year raised enough money to resume work on the Gothic building. It was completed, with the exception of the towers, on March 4, 1917.

The most devastating incident in the cathedral's history took place November 26, 1975, when the building was struck by an arsonist. The largest and most costly fire in Topeka history gutted the edifice, leaving only the walls standing.

Reconstruction began almost immediately. Services were held in the basement of the Great Hall and remained there until October 1, 1978, when the reconstructed cathedral was ready for use.

Work continues toward completion of the cathedral. New stained glass windows have been installed around the altar, in the nave and transepts. The rose windows in each transept were installed in 1989 and dedicated in 1990. The most recent additions were two windows in the clerestory in 1992. A new cathedra and clergy chairs were installed in 1987.

The design of the roof resembles English parish churches with its oak-covered steel trusses supported on hammer beams. The trusses are supported by column capitals of handcarved stone.

The pulpit, altar, chancel rail and other appointments are temporary replacements.

Oklahoma

Southwest

St. Paul's Cathedral,
Oklahoma City

St. Paul's celebrated its centennial recently, recalling the founding of a small congregation just after Oklahoma's Great Land Run of 1889.

A group of 10 persons organized St. Paul's in January, 1891, and met in several places, including a federal court room, until 1893, when its first building was erected. The original wood frame structure was located in what is now downtown Oklahoma City and later was moved to another site.

The parish soon outgrew its church and purchased land for a new building. The cornerstone for the present cathedral was laid during the summer of 1903, and the first service in the new building, designed by Arthur J. Williams, was held March 13, 1904.

When Oklahoma became a state in 1907, St. Paul's parishioners constructed a house and invited Francis K. Brooke, first Bishop of Oklahoma, to move from Guthrie and make his residence there. St. Paul's also requested to be designated as the cathedral, and in 1908, this took place.

The parish house was constructed in 1909, and the Cathedral Center in 1949. A seven-arch cloister and garden connect the church to the Cathedral Center.

St. Paul's is of Norman Gothic design in the tradition of an English country church. There is a characteristic square Norman bell tower which has never had a bell. The brick and stone church has a gabled roof supported by wooden beams. The ends of those beams have unusual ram heads which conceal roof reinforcers. White plaster walls conceal an arch of brick between chancel and nave.

The altar and reredos were executed in Italy from Carrara marble and were installed in 1927. The altar is the work of Domano D'Orestes of Florence, who followed the design of Leonard H. Bailey. The large pulpit, installed in 1925, also is of marble. A marble baptismal font is located opposite the pulpit, and a wooden Madonna and eagle lectern are nearby. The bishop's throne, to the left of the altar, has a finely-carved canopy.

St. Paul's has 38 stained glass windows which tell the story of Christ and the spreading of Christianity.

Two Tiffany windows are found in the apse, on both sides of the reredos. They were installed in 1903 when the church was built, and represent Christ the Good Shepherd and the Ascension. There are six windows set in dormers featuring angels with Christian symbols.

Windows in the nave are in the form of three triptychs on each side. Windows on the west side depict the ministries of St. John, St. Paul and St. Luke. On the east side are portrayals of the Nativity, Crucifixion and Resurrection.

The window above the narthex entrance depicts the Te Deum, with Christ in Majesty the subject of the center panel. Narthex windows depict the lives of the apostles; others illustrate the ministry of the patron saint, Paul.

The Chapel of St. Nicholas, intended for children, is located in the Cathedral Center.

The cathedral's organ is a three-manual, 41-rank Aeolian-Skinner instrument which includes antiphonal trumpets on the narthex wall below the Te Deum window.

St. John's Cathedral,
Albuquerque

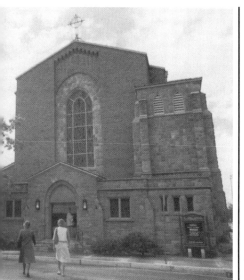

The Rio Grande
Southwest

One of the newer buildings among American cathedrals is St. John's, which was dedicated in 1952.

The first Episcopal service in Albuquerque was held March 4, 1875, in a hotel room, when William F. Adams, Bishop of the Missionary District of New Mexico and Arizona, was present, along with his chaplain, Henry Forrester.

A highlight of that first service was the ordination of Territorial Supreme Court Justice Hezekiah S. Johnson, one of the nine persons in that congregation, as a deacon.

In October, 1880, when Bishop George Dunlop moved his headquarters from Albuquerque to Las Vegas, Forrester returned to Albuquerque and helped the little congregation prepare for the future. Forrester secured a site for a building, and donations were obtained.

A building of Arizona sandstone was constructed, and St. John's was opened November 5, 1882. Financial problems plagued the congregation, and it wasn't until 1894 that the building could be consecrated and the debt paid off. St. John's achieved parish status January 24, 1900.

At that time, St. John's was part of the District of New Mexico and Southwest Texas, since Arizona had become a district of its own in 1892.

Bishop Frederick B. Howden was consecrated in 1914, and decided to make Albuquerque rather than El Paso his see city. In 1920, a proposal was made to establish St. John's as the cathedral of the district. A Cathedral Foundation was formed on an experimental basis for a year, and St. John's was recognized as a pro-cathedral for seven years. It achieved cathedral status in 1927.

A parish house was constructed in the early 1930s and improvements were made to the cathedral as well.

Albuquerque experienced considerable growth in the late 1940s, and St. John's supported the creation of two new missions. In 1951, a decision was made to build a new cathedral, and the architectural firm of Meem, Zehner, Holien and Associates was selected.

The foundation stone was laid November 25, 1951. The building was of brick in a Gothic style typical of southern France but incorporating elements of Anglican tradition in a lofty nave and chancel, with low side aisles and a flanking chapel. The wood ceiling was English Gothic, containing colored panels between the beams. Stone from the old church was used for the foundations, facade and side entrance. The tower from the old church was taken down, then rebuilt into the northwest corner of the new building.

On September 11, 1952, while the building was under construction, the missionary district became the Diocese of New Mexico and Southwest Texas. The new cathedral was dedicated November 11, 1952 during the first convention of the new diocese, with Presiding Bishop Henry K. Sherrill present. The building was consecrated April 23, 1963, also during convention. The name of the diocese was changed to the Diocese of the Rio Grande in 1973.

All the cathedral's stained glass windows were installed by 1976 and executed by Connick and Company of Boston. The largest is the Great North Window, installed in 1963. The three windows above the high altar depict the Crucifixion, Ascension and Resurrection. The nave windows portray various scenes from the Bible, and the Apostles appear in the choir clerestory windows.

The Diocese of the Rio Grande also has a pro-cathedral, St. Clement's, in El Paso, Texas. El Paso had been the see city of Southwest Texas before it merged with New Mexico to form the new Rio Grande diocese.

Texas
Southwest

Although the idea of a cathedral for the Diocese of Texas was discussed as early as 1873, it was 1949 before Christ Church, Houston, achieved cathedral status.

Christ Church existed for more than 100 years before it took on its new role. It was the first church in Houston and is the only one continuing to worship on its original site from the days when Houston was the capital of the Republic of Texas.

The city of Houston was started in 1837, and two years later a paper was signed to organize a congregation. That paper attracted 28 signers, and 45 persons pledged support. Land was acquired, and a brick church built in 1845. The building was consecrated in 1847 by George W. Freeman, Bishop of the Southwest, who had provisional charge of the church in Texas.

The congregation grew rapidly, and soon outgrew its little building. In 1859, the cornerstone was laid for a second church. An interesting tale recalls that as the new building was being laid out, a cattleman driving a herd past the site stopped to ask workers what they were doing. When he was told that a church was going to be built, he roped a steer and donated it as a contribution. A steer's head is now part of the diocesan seal.

Construction was slowed by the Civil War, but it was reported in 1866 that the new church would soon be ready for consecration. In the same year it was described as too small. The church was enlarged in time for Easter Day, 1876.

The idea of a cathedral came up in 1873, when it was discussed by the Diocesan Council. The idea was rejected because of the vast geographic area of the Diocese of Texas. The diocese was divided the following year, but the cathedral proposal was not brought to the Diocesan Council again until 1929.

In 1893, while workers were trying to connect the new cloister to the church, a wall fell. It was decided to build a new church rather than undertake costly repairs.

The new building, designed by J. Arthur Tempest and Silas McBee, was ready for services on Christmas Eve, 1893. The edifice, now the cathedral, was built in the Gothic revival style.

Bishop Clinton S. Quin brought up the subject of a cathedral again in 1929 in his first address to Diocesan Council. He mentioned it again in his 1931 address, and the matter was turned over to a committee for a report in 1932. Again the matter was delayed, and then, because of the Great Depression, the possibility seemed all but forgotten.

Bishop Quin's next public mention of a cathedral was during his 1940 address to Diocesan Council, when he said he was ready to designate a parish church as the cathedral. World War II delayed the matter again. Finally, in 1947, Christ Church offered itself as the cathedral. Two years later Diocesan Council approved, and on February 6, 1949, during the centennial celebration of the Diocese of Texas, Bishop Quin proclaimed Christ Church the cathedral.

In 1938 an adjacent office building caught fire. Flames swept through the chancel, and the roof collapsed over the altar. While battling the blaze, a fireman sprayed the rood screen in an attempt to save it. The screen still stands, with minor charring visible when on the altar side.

Other buildings have been added to the complex, forming a U-shape around a grass-covered court in downtown Houston. Work began on the diocesan offices and the Latham Memorial Building in 1950 along with renovation of the Guild Hall. The Chapel of the Christ Child was opened in late 1953, and Cleveland Hall was built in 1961.

*Grace and Holy
Trinity Cathedral,
Kansas City*

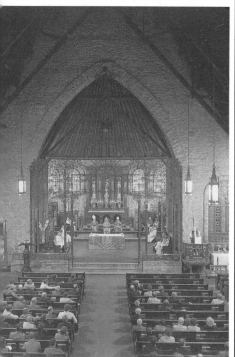

West Missouri
Southwest

Kansas City's cathedral has endured a serious fire and the collapse of one of its walls. As its name implies, Grace and Holy Trinity is the result of a merger of parishes.

Its foundation occurred July 20, 1870, when St. Paul's parish was organized and began meeting in the basement of an opera house.[5] On April 14, 1873, the congregation adopted the name Grace Church and made plans for a church building. That building was used for the first time on Christmas Day, 1874.

Kansas City began to grow rapidly, and by 1887 plans were being made to build another church. In 1889, the foundation for a new building, the present cathedral, was laid. In May of that year, the Diocese of Missouri was divided, creating the Diocese of West Missouri.

The first service in the new Grace Church was held December 16, 1894, and the building was consecrated by E.R. Atwell, first Bishop of West Missouri, May 15, 1898.

Trinity Church was the second founding parish. Its first services were held in 1883 in a room over a meat market. A lot was purchased the following year and construction began on a place of worship. The Romanesque building was completed in 1888. The congregation never could retire the debt from construction, and when Grace Church was without a rector in 1917, the two churches decided to merge. The name Grace and Holy Trinity was adopted and Grace Church was used for services.

In 1929, the church was struck by fire during the middle of Holy Week. The organ had been electrified the previous week, and while a student was practicing at the organ, flames were seen coming from the organ pipes. The fire left the floor charred and some of the windows were damaged.[6]

Bishop Robert Spencer, a former rector of the parish, was in favor of a cathedral, and on May 14, 1935, the Diocesan Convention accepted Grace and Holy Trinity as the cathedral.

A bell tower, which had been capped at 35 feet when the church was constructed, was completed to a height of 72 feet, and bells rang for the first time on Easter Day, 1938.

In 1985, renovation of the interior was discussed but no action was taken. Then, on January 22, 1986, a portion of the outside north wall collapsed, causing significant damage, and forcing services to be moved to the parish hall for 20 months. In September of that year, renovation was begun. It included repair of the walls, rafters and roofs, restoration of the bell tower and floors, enlargement of the baptismal area and relocation of the altar. That work was completed in 1987.

The cathedral is of transitional Norman style, designed by Frederick E. Hill and constructed of native limestone.

Some of the finest stained glass windows are found in the chancel apse area. They were made by Powell and Sons of London and installed after the fire of 1929. They depict the Annunciation, Nativity, Baptism, Crucifixion, Resurrection and Ascension. The Tiffany Hart window, at the west balcony, is the largest and highest of the cathedral's windows. The original window was destroyed in the fire of 1929, but Tiffany's was able to reproduce the original, and it was installed in 1930. A small crescent-shaped window at the rear of the church contains the symbols of Grace and the Trinity.

The high altar, carved of oak by Edward Roemer, has been in the building since its construction. The reredos, set in the apse, was installed in 1992. It is made of Tennessee red oak and has three panels painted in 1939 by James Roth, showing St. Peter, Christ blessing and St. John the Evangelist. The bronze pulpit was a gift to the cathedral in 1909.

Western Louisiana
Southwest

After 150 years as a parish church, St. Mark's was set apart as a cathedral in 1990.

St. Mark's goes back to 1839, when Leonidas Polk, Missionary Bishop of Arkansas, held the first Episcopal service in Shreveport. The actual incorporation of the parish didn't occur until 12 years later, when Grace Church became known as St. Mark's on April 22, 1851. After worshiping in various locations, the congregation had the first building of its own in 1859.

By the end of the 19th century, there was agreement among the parishioners that a need existed for a new and larger church.[7] Property was purchased in 1900 and a cornerstone was laid May 22, 1904. The first service in the new Gothic building designed by C.W. Bulger was held April 9, 1905.

On December 10, 1919, fire caused considerable damage to the church, with estimates of damage as high as $30,000.[8] Most parish records were destroyed and the roof had to be rebuilt. A Jewish temple offered its building for worship while rebuilding took place.

The parish showed steady growth during the next three decades, and in the late 1940s, plans were made to become involved in a long-range building program in the suburban Fairfield area. Phase one, which involved construction of a parish hall, began with groundbreaking April 27, 1952. That project was finished in 1954, providing rooms for Sunday school classes and parish offices. That building also served as worship space from 1954-59.

Phase two, the construction of the main church building, began in 1956. The architectural firm of Annan and Gilmer designed a 14th century Gothic building with a tower modeled after that of Magdalen College in Oxford.[9] The present church was completed in June, 1959, but the first service was held a month earlier, on May 3. It was dedicated September 15, 1959 by Bishop Girault M. Jones of Louisiana, and consecrated November 6, 1962.

All the furnishings were new except the high altar, communion rail, font and lectern, which were brought from the second St. Mark's.

The third phase of the building program was construction of the day school building, which began in March, 1978, and was completed in July, 1979.

In 1979, the Diocese of Louisiana was divided, and St. Mark's became part of the new Diocese of Western Louisiana. At that time, Alexandria was the see city of the new diocese.

On July 7, 1990, St. Mark's was set apart as a cathedral by Willis R. Henton, first Bishop of Western Louisiana. His successor, Robert J. Hargrove, was seated at the same service.

St. Mark's has many interesting stained glass windows. Most of them were designed and manufactured in London by J. Wippell and Co. Ltd., with the exception of the great west window, the rose window and two in the chapel, which were designed by the Judson Studios of Los Angeles.

In the nave there are windows on the lower level and the clerestory level. Those of interest include a series on the right side of the building symbolizing the seven sacraments. The front window of that series portrays the baptism of an infant George Washington and includes the letters GW.[10]

The great west window depicts the Ascension and Baptism of Christ, and the rose window above the altar has a chalice at the center with symbols of the apostles in the "petals." The large window in the north transept shows the Nativity and the Presentation of Christ in the temple. The south transept window depicts the Crucifixion and Resurrection.

Mid Atlantic

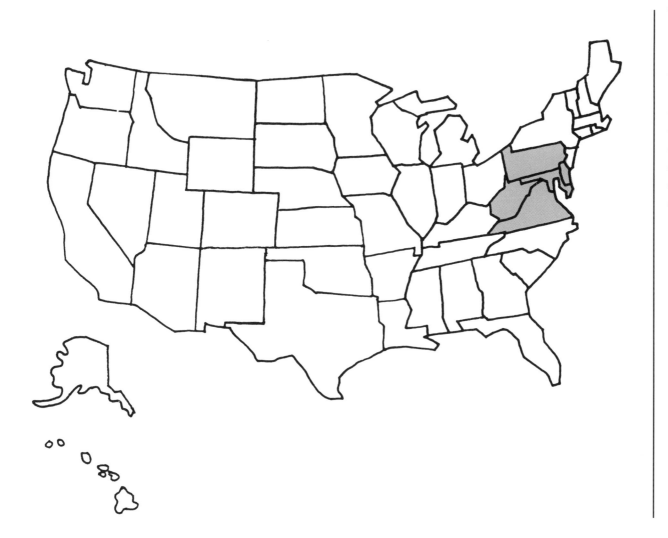

The Dioceses of

Washington
Bethlehem
Central Pennsylvania
Delaware
Easton
Maryland
Northwestern Pennsylvania
Pennsylvania
Pittsburgh

Washington
Mid Atlantic

Washington National Cathedral is probably the best-known of Episcopal cathedrals, receiving thousands of visitors each year and having its Christmas services televised nationally. The cathedral was completed in 1989, and is the sixth largest in the world.

The possibility of a cathedral in the federal capital was discussed as early as 1792 by Thomas Clagett, the first Bishop of Maryland, but it was a century before the idea gained momentum.

In 1893, Congress granted a charter to establish a cathedral in Washington, and the following year the Diocese of Washington was formed. Henry Y. Saterlee, first Bishop of Washington, raised more than $300,000 and purchased 57 acres on Mt. St. Alban in the northwest section of Washington. By 1898 the property had been acquired free of all debt.

British architect George F. Bodley was commissioned in 1906 to draw plans for a cathedral with the assistance of Henry Vaughan of Boston. Bodley died in 1907 and Vaughan continued on the project until his death in 1917. Bodley's plans for a building based on 14th century English Gothic design to be constructed of Indiana limestone were approved in June, 1907. On September 29 of that year, President Theodore Roosevelt laid the foundation stone, which came from a field near Bethlehem.

Bethlehem Chapel was the first portion of the cathedral to be completed, opening in 1912 for services which have continued daily ever since. Construction was halted in 1919 because of World War I, and wasn't resumed until 1921. In that year, Philip H. Frohman, E. Donald Robb and Harry B. Little, partners in a Boston architectural firm, were designated cathedral architects. Robb continued until his death in 1942, Little until he died in 1944.

Work on the choir began in 1922 and continued for a decade. In 1928, the Episcopal Church's General Convention was opened at the cathedral by President Calvin Coolidge and a service was held on the main level, even though it was without a roof. The chancel was opened on Easter Day, 1932, with a temporary wall.

Construction was slowed, yet continued during the Depression, but it was stopped during the early part of World War II. Following the war, work began on the south transept, which was completed in 1962. The 676-foot central tower, the only one in the world to contain both bells and a carillon, was dedicated in 1964 and is the highest point in Washington.

The nave was enclosed by 1972 as the north and south walls met at the west facade. The completed nave was dedicated in 1976 in a series of ceremonies attended by, among others, Queen Elizabeth II, President Gerald Ford and Archbishop of Canterbury Donald Coggan.

When a shortage of funds occurred in 1977, construction stopped again for three years. The Pilgrim Observation Gallery was completed following resumption and opened to the public in 1982. Work stopped again until April 5, 1983 when the first stone for the west towers was set. Completion ceremonies were held in September, 1990, marking the end of 83 years of construction.

The first completed entrance is in the north transept. Niches in the porch entrance contain carvings of female saints. The south transept entrance features a carving of the Last Supper above the entrance, a large statue of St. Alban and 44 angel figures carved over the entrance.

The principal entrance to the cathedral is through the west facade, designed by Frohman, last architect of the cathedral. The bronze gates are from German sculptor Ulrich Henn and were cast in England. Creation is the theme of the facade, which features a carved typanum showing the creation of humanity. The narthex floor is a mosaic made up of state seals.

The nave includes bays which carry out various themes. Just inside the west entrance is the Washington Bay, dominated by a 7-foot-6-inch statue of George Washington made of Vermont marble. The Warren Bay is found along the south aisle and is accompanied by the space window, which commemorates the flight of Apollo XI. The window contains a sliver of moon rock brought back from that flight. Also on the south aisle is the Woodrow Wilson Bay, which includes the tomb of President Wilson.

Bays on the north side include the Kellogg Bay, which contains a statue of Martin Luther King Jr., and the Abraham Lincoln Bay, which has a marble floor inset with Lincoln-head pennies in a shield.

A statue of Samuel Seabury, the first Bishop of the Episcopal Church, is found in the south transept vestibule. The statue is the work of sculptor Theodore Barbarossa. The south transept also has a fine rose window illustrating the church triumphant. Opposite, in the north transept, is another rose window, depicting the last judgment.

Another rose window is the magnificent one (25 feet, 11 inches in diameter) at the west end of the building by Rowan LeCompte, which has a theme of the creation of light.

Washington Cathedral is the only one in the world which is the seat of two bishops—the Bishop of Washington and the Presiding Bishop of the Episcopal Church. There are three cathedras: The Glastonbury cathedra, made of stones from Glastonbury Abbey, England, may be used by any bishop taking part in a service. The other two cathedras are on each side in the choir stalls at the ends nearest the altar.[1]

The high altar is known as the Jerusalem Altar because it is made of stone from quarries near Jerusalem.[2] It is topped by a magnificent stone reredos, which has 110 carved statues of prominent figures of Christianity with Christ in Majesty at the center.

Two windows at the east end of the cathedral have the theme Te Deum. The windows are 65 feet high and designed by Earl Edward Sanborn.

The four enormous piers at the crossing are 98 feet high to the vaulting and are 19 feet in diameter.

Nearby furnishings of interest are the choir stalls, carved in oak; the Canterbury pulpit, made of stones from Canterbury Cathedral; and the lectern, carved of Indiana limestone.

There are many chapels in the cathedral, including five on the main floor and four in the crypt. St. Mary's Chapel has an elaborate linden wood reredos and 16th century Flemish tapestries which tell the story of David and Goliath. Holy Spirit Chapel is set aside for private prayer and meditation. St. John's Chapel has an attractive reredos and carved bosses in the vaulting. Other chapels on this floor are War Memorial and Children's.

In the crypt are Bethlehem Chapel; St. Joseph of Arimathea Chapel, with an interesting mural painting; the Chapel of the Resurrection; and the Chapel of the Good Shepherd.

The organ was built by Ernest M. Skinner of Methuen, Massachusetts, in 1938 and has 126 stops and more than 8,300 pipes.

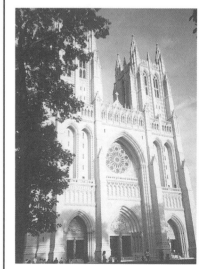

Bethlehem

Mid Atlantic

The Cathedral of the Nativity existed as a pro-cathedral for more than 50 years before achieving cathedral status. And before taking on its role as a pro-cathedral for the eastern Pennsylvania diocese, it was a parish church for more than 30 years.

Episcopalians in Bethlehem in the 1850s began to gather for worship wherever they could find a place to meet. On May 6, 1862, a small group met in a home and decided to organize a congregation. A lot was purchased and the Episcopalians began to hold worship services in a Moravian chapel.

In August, 1863, a cornerstone was laid for a new building, designed by Edward T. Potter. The first service in the English Gothic-style edifice was held on Christmas Day, 1864. William Stevens, Bishop of Pennsylvania, consecrated the church April 19, 1865.

The Church of the Nativity was described at the time of its consecration as being of "rural Gothic style," with buttressed stone walls, deep, narrow lancet windows, slate roof and bell gable surmounted by a stone cross.[3]

By 1884 it was necessary to enlarge the church. It was decided to construct a new chancel and nave across the original building, retaining east and west ends intact, thus forming transepts. Through this construction, nothing of the original edifice was lost, since it was incorporated within the larger church.[4] Instead of the nave running west to east as it had, it now ran from south to north.

The new church was ready for use on Christmas Day, 1887, and was consecrated a year later on November 1, All Saints' Day. A parish house was added in 1896.

When Ethelbert Talbot was enthroned as Bishop of the Diocese of Bethlehem February 2, 1899, the Church of the Nativity became the pro-cathedral.

Fifty-one years later, in 1950, Nativity was designated as the cathedral.

A major renovation took place the following year. Walls and foundations were strengthened, the parish house renovated, the organ cleaned and plumbing and heating improved.

A major feature of the interior of the cathedral is the rood screen with its brass cross and angels, dating to 1899. The marble altar was made free-standing in 1985. The handsomely-carved cathedra was presented as a gift before the Church of the Nativity achieved pro-cathedral status.

Throughout the chancel and transepts are interesting needlepoint designs which were created by women of the cathedral.

Many of the stained glass windows were installed in the original church. The rose window over the entrance has a shield in the center depicting Christ's protection of his people. Each "petal" of the rose honors a saint. The clerestory windows to the east present a panorama of significant developments in the history of both Nativity and Bethlehem, from the arrival of William Penn to the local steel industry. The Nativity window in the east transept was over the altar before the church was renovated and took on its present shape.

Nativity has had a renowned choir of men and boys for more than 100 years.

Central Pennsylvania
Mid Atlantic

St. Stephen's Cathedral, Harrisburg

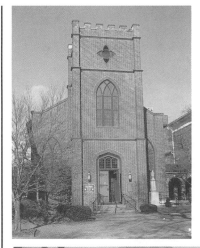

St. Stephen's is one of the oldest buildings among Episcopal cathedrals, dating back to 1826. It existed as a parish church for more than 100 years before achieving cathedral status.

Regular Episcopal services began in Harrisburg in 1823 and were led by visiting clergy. In 1826, it became clear that a church was needed in Pennsylvania's capital city, and the Rev. John B. Clemson took services, beginning February 15. The first vestry meeting was held the following month, and plans were made in April for a church building.

The cornerstone for that building was laid June 24, 1826. St. Stephen's was consecrated May 9, 1827, by the Rt. Rev. William White during the convention of the Diocese of Pennsylvania. Parish records show the little congregation incurred financial problems during the early years, and reached a crisis in 1828, when the vestry minutes tell of the possibility that the church might "to go to the hammer."[5]

The financial problems eased during the next decade, and both the congregation and the building soon began to grow. A rectory was built in 1855, and a mission church grew out of St. Stephen's two years later.

In 1860, the church was lengthened 12 feet, new pews and windows were installed, and alterations were made to the rectory. A Sunday school building, which later became the parish house, was constructed behind the church.

The north side of the chancel was enlarged in 1880, and in 1894 a new chancel was built and the ceiling of the nave paneled with wood. By the end of 1900, an annex joined the church and parish house, providing an extra classroom and vesting space for clergy and choir. The rectory was sold in 1915, and the property beside the church, now known as Cathedral House, was purchased.

In 1871 the Diocese of Central Pennsylvania was created out of the Diocese of Pennsylvania and its first convention was held at St. Stephen's. In 1904 Central Pennsylvania was divided, creating the Diocese of Harrisburg, and in 1931 Bishop Wyatt Hunter-Brown made St. Stephen's Harrisburg's cathedral.

Central Pennsylvania was later renamed the Diocese of Bethlehem, and in 1971 Harrisburg, to avoid confusion with the Roman Catholic Diocese of Harrisburg, adopted the then unused title, Central Pennsylvania.

The cathedral's stained glass windows were repaired in 1948 and again in 1974. The undercroft was excavated in 1950 to provide classrooms and meeting space, and a new deanery was purchased in 1955. The church was redecorated in 1964, providing a bishop's throne, hanging cross and new light fixtures.

Flags of various jurisdictions are hanging in the nave. On one side are the flags of civil entities which have affected Harrisburg, and on the other side are flags from ecclesiastical jurisdictions. Among them is a flag of the Anglican Communion, believed to be one of only two in existence. The other is in the possession of the Archbishop of Canterbury.

The stained glass windows at St. Stephen's were installed at various times and executed by a variety of studios. Among those of interest are one of the cathedral's patron, St. Stephen, near the font, and illustrations of St. John the Evangelist and St. Faith near the lectern. Among the new windows installed above the choir in 1990 is one which pictures the Susquehanna River flowing through Harrisburg.

The cathedral is well-known outside its diocese for its annual Seminar on Prayer and Healing, now in its 31st year. The seminar draws about 500 participants from all over the world each year in May.

Delaware

Mid Atlantic

Delaware's handsome cathedral occupies the site once held by a tavern of notorious reputation.

A meeting was held August 7, 1855 to organize a parish, and the name St. John's was chosen. A year later, the congregation purchased the site then occupied by the Green Tree Inn, a tavern which had existed there since Revolutionary War days, and was "reputed to be a place of vilest wickedness."[6] A brick building was erected to serve as a chapel and Sunday school, and it was opened December 27, 1856.

A cornerstone was laid for a new church building June 13, 1857, by Alfred Lee, first Bishop of Delaware. The edifice, which is the present cathedral, was consecrated November 3, 1858, and pews were to be free, an unusual declaration for that time.[7]

Among the traditions of St. John's is a story, without proof, that the high altar of the cathedral stands on the very spot where the bar of the Green Tree Inn once stood.[8]

The Gothic church was designed by John Notman of Philadelphia, constructed of Brandywine blue granite, and topped by an imposing tower and steeple.

The original church school building was torn down in 1885 and a new stone building erected.

A major expansion of church property took place in 1920. More classrooms were added, a larger auditorium constructed, a rectory built on the church grounds, the chancel was extended, and St. Mary's Chapel was created. The cornerstone was placed in the wall of the chapel March 13, 1920, and the new buildings were consecrated May 5, 1921, by Philip Cook, Bishop of Delaware.

St. John's was established as the cathedral May 14, 1935, when Bishop Cook addressed the diocesan convention meeting at St. John's.

During the years 1961-67, a program of rehabilitation of the buildings was carried out, involving repairing and strengthening the walls and roof beams, and replastering and decorating the interior. Additional work was done in 1989.

Among the interesting stained glass windows in St. John's is one above the altar which depicts the Last Supper. The window was made in Europe and shipped to the United States. Everything except the supper scene was damaged beyond repair during shipping, and the work above and below it in the window was added much later.

The great west window dominates the nave and includes, eclectic in theme, scenes from the life of Christ, a dirigible, a train, the Washington Monument and the Empire State Building. The small window in the west wall of the south transept illustrates incidents in the Christian nature of a child, and is considered by many to be the finest in the cathedral. This window, and many of the others in the cathedral, were executed by the Henry L. Willet Studios of Philadelphia.

On the north side of the north transept is the original door of St. John's, dating to 1857. The door is not hinged, but turns on metal pivots set into the upper and lower frames.

The south transept contains the baptistry with its white Caen stone font.

St. Mary's Chapel contains some interesting furnishings, including the screen which has a variety of carved musical instruments. The reredos behind the altar contains sculpted figures of the Virgin Mary at the Annunciation, the Nativity, the Presentation and the Crucifixion. The windows portray women in the Bible and are the work of the d'Ascenso Studio of Philadelphia.

Easton
Mid Atlantic

The Gothic cathedral in Easton is certainly one of the smallest in the Episcopal Church, and serves the diocese which covers Maryland's Eastern Shore.

The Diocese of Easton was created in 1868 out of the Diocese of Maryland, and Henry C. Lay became its first bishop. At that time, Christ Church was the only Episcopal church in Easton, having been founded in 1800. Christ Church had a handsome building designed by William Strickland of Philadelphia and consecrated in 1848, but Bishop Lay felt a cathedral should be built for the young diocese.

Bishop Lay spoke at length of the need for a cathedral at the diocesan convention of 1874, when he argued that a bishop needed more than a parish church for the center of his ministry. Two years later, articles of incorporation under Maryland law were granted for Trinity Cathedral. Bishop Lay urged the diocesan convention of 1876 to pursue the cathedral idea further. He also proposed such institutions as schools, orphanages and a library as being natural near a cathedral. Trinity was incorporated June 20 of that year and a small frame chapel seating 150 was erected to serve as a temporary cathedral. It opened for services September 24, 1876, and was voted into admission by the diocesan convention in 1877.

The congregation which worshiped in the small building grew steadily, and funds were raised for a larger stone structure with a French slate roof. The present cathedral held its first worship service July 5, 1891.[9] It was consecrated May 23, 1894, by the Rt. Rev. William F. Adams. The original plan called for a close, library, episcopal residence, deanery and chapter house, but only the cathedral itself was built.

Even though construction ended, the cathedral, in the minds of many, was not complete. "In a real sense, the work of building the cathedral church should never cease," the diocesan newspaper said. "Even now the chancel is inadequate for great occasions. The sanctuary is not sufficiently large for ordinations."[10]

Trinity is of traditional Gothic design in gray granite from Port Deposit, Maryland, with a bell tower, which was not completed until 1978. The tower was not built according to the original design because the plans reportedly were lost, so a new tower was designed by Bryden Bordley Hyde of Baltimore. The bell in that tower came from All Saints' Church after that parish was closed. An odd feature of the building is its apse, which is typically French and found in only a few places in England.

The church contains some fine stained glass windows picturing New Testament scenes. The brass altar cross, of Greek design, also is noteworthy. It is original to the cathedral, as are most of the appointments, and has medallions in its face which shown scenes of the life and works of Jesus. There is a striking set of stations of the cross, which were painted in watercolor by Susan Norton-Taylor May. The interior was restored twice during the past 25 years.

Among the stained glass windows are two in the sanctuary which were dedicated in 1973. One depicts St. Luke and the other St. Matthew, both shown carrying the gospels they wrote.

An important guest visited Trinity in 1981. The Archbishop of Canterbury, Robert A.K. Runcie, came to Trinity in connection with the observance of the 350th anniversary of the first church of the Anglican Communion in America, dating from Capt. William Claiborne's settlement on Kent Island in 1631.

Maryland
Mid Atlantic

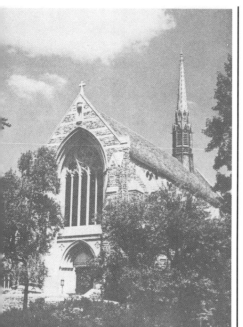

The Diocese of Maryland's mother church is an unfinished building. While records indicate there were Anglican services in Maryland as early as 1632, it was 150 years before there was a Diocese of Maryland, and 300 years before there was a cathedral.

Legislation toward the creation of a cathedral began in 1908, when the convention of the diocese set up a cathedral board of trustees upon a recommendation by Bishop William Paret. One year later, a 3.63-acre site was purchased, and another adjoining acre was acquired in 1910.

Henry Vaughan of Boston, architect of Washington Cathedral, was authorized to prepare a preliminary sketch of a first unit of the cathedral group, a synod hall, a building designed for use as a church until the cathedral itself should be built.[11]

Ground was broken for the undercroft of the new building on December 9, 1909, and Bishop John G. Murray established residence in a home on the newly-acquired property.

Meanwhile, the merged parish churches of St. Barnabas and St. George agreed to become the nucleus of the cathedral venture. The two congregations turned over their entire resources and sacrificed their parochial identities, which dated back to 1863 and 1875, respectively.[12]

Those churches had purchased a lot for a new building, which they sold for $14,500. They added $15,000, and the trustees of the Cathedral Foundation applied the entire amount toward the purchase of land. Other parishes of the diocese also contributed until more than $54,000 was on hand to take over 4.69 acres free of all encumbrance.[13]

The cathedral's first service was held June 11, 1911, Trinity Sunday, in the undercroft, attended mostly by members of the St. Barnabas and St. George congregations.[14]

When World War I broke out, construction nearly stopped for almost a decade, but other developments occurred. In 1920, a group of Baltimore financiers decided to raise by private means the sum necessary to complete the first building, Synod Hall, which was usually referred to as the pro-cathedral. The cornerstone was laid by Bishop Murray November 11, 1920. Construction forced the congregation to move to a temporary frame building nearby.

Setbacks delayed further construction. Underground streams were discovered, a drainage problem occurred, and funds became difficult to acquire in the post-war period. Work was suspended, and the congregation returned to the undercroft, where it worshiped for 10 more years.

Work resumed November 11, 1931, an occasion marked by a service led by Bishop Edward Helfenstein.[15]

From there, construction went according to schedule. The congregation filled all 500 seats and many were standing when the first service was held on Christmas Eve, 1932.[16]

Synod Hall was originally designed by Bertram G. Goodhue, architect of the Cathedral of St. John the Divine in New York City, and was built of stone. Goodhue died before the building could be completed, and Philip Frohman was engaged to design the building.

On February 1, 1955, the Diocese of Maryland passed a resolution establishing the Cathedral Church of the Incarnation and removing the title pro-cathedral.

The cathedral contains many stained glass windows of note, 10 of which were designed by Henry Willet of the Willet Studio of Philadelphia. The Nativity window over the altar includes seven panels and depicts incidents which surround the birth of Christ. The large window at the west end is known as the Easter window and depicts events leading up to the Resurrection. It was designed by Joseph Reynolds of Boston.

Northwestern Pennsylvania
Mid Atlantic

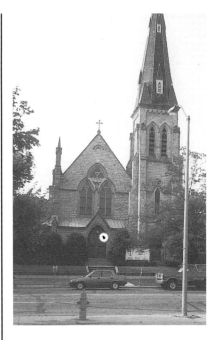

St. Paul's has stood on the same site for more than 150 years, first as a small, brick church, then as a larger building which eventually became a cathedral.

Episcopal ministry began in Erie in 1826, when the Rev. J.H. Hopkins of Pittsburgh held services in the court house. The parish was organized March 17, 1827, at a meeting held in a house. The congregation's first church was a brick building with a wooden tower, which was consecrated in 1834.

The present cathedral was built in 1866 on the same site, but did not include the planned spire, which later was given by a vestryman. George W. Lloyd was architect of the gray, stone Gothic edifice, which was consecrated July 29, 1866.

Fire damaged the building in 1881 as a result of a sexton trying to make an adjustment inside the organ. He used a candle, which ignited some material, causing destruction of the organ and other damage to the church, including the reredos, which had to be redecorated.

In 1910, the Diocese of Erie was created out of the Diocese of Pittsburgh. The first Bishop of Erie, Rogers Israel, designated St. Paul's as the cathedral of the new diocese in 1915, and the vestry was reconstituted as a chapter. Changes also were made in the charter to reflect the cathedral status.[17]

The Diocese of Erie was renamed the Diocese of Northwestern Pennsylvania in 1974.

The construction of new buildings and the acquisition of others added to the cathedral complex. A parish house was erected in 1900 and a chapter house, which includes an auditorium, classrooms and office space, was added in 1928. In addition, a rectory was purchased and another nearby home acquired.

There have been two major renovation and improvement projects. The first began in 1932 and continued for 20 years, with an interruption by World War II. The project was planned and directed by J. Ellsworth Potter of Cleveland and was completed with a dedication service June 1, 1952. The second project took place in 1983 and brought additional rehabilitation along with the installation of a new pipe organ.

St. Paul's faces north, with the main entrance through a narthex, separated from the nave by a wall. Another entrance is on the west side of the building.

The older windows in the cathedral are the work of the J & R Lamb Studios of Spring Valley, New York. Those installed after 1935 were designed and executed by the Henry L. Willet Studios of Philadelphia. Among the windows of note is the large one at the north end, built around the prayer book canticles Benedicite and Te Deum. The 12 round windows in the clerestory contain symbols of the Apostles, with the exception of Judas, who was replaced by St. Paul. The window above the reredos depicts Christ as a healer. It is believed this window was made in Austria. One window was made by the Tiffany Studio and others are done in the Tiffany style.

The altar is of white marble with the front containing the symbols of Alpha and Omega. The reredos and chancel are of dark carved oak, with the figure of Christ as the Light of the World. Some of the wood below the figure of Christ came from Oliver Hazard Perry's ship, the *Niagara*, flagship of the Battle of Lake Erie during the War of 1812.

The south wall contains lifesize painted figures of St. Paul and the four evangelists. That wall was damaged in the fire of 1881 and once bore inscriptions of the Lord's Prayer, Creed and Ten Commandments.

Pennsylvania
Mid Atlantic

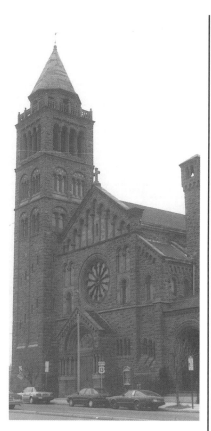

One of the newest cathedrals in the Episcopal Church is the large Romanesque building on the west side of Philadelphia, which became Pennsylvania's cathedral January 1, 1992. Church of the Saviour received this designation after a plan to build a church of a size comparable to European-size cathedrals failed early in the 20th century.

The Church of the Saviour existed as a parish for more than 140 years before the Rt. Rev. Allen L. Bartlett, Jr. proposed making it the cathedral. He recommended the Saviour as the best cathedral site in 1990, then reached agreement with the church's vestry in October, 1991.

The parish had a meager beginning, with a small group meeting October 11, 1850, to organize a congregation. The group chose Church of the Good Shepherd as its name, but eight days later changed it to Church of the Saviour. The cornerstone for a small wooden building was laid October 11, 1852, but by 1854 the building had been abandoned because the church proved to be inaccessible to the many who wanted to become members.[18]

The location of the present building was obtained in July, 1855, and construction began in October of that year on a new church. The first service in the stone building was in the "lecture room" on Thanksgiving Day, 1856, and the church itself was opened in April, 1857.

Extensive renovations were done to the church in 1889, including an enlargement of the building and the erection of the present facade and tower. Three years later, a disastrous fire destroyed all but the front of the building. Services were held in the nearby Drexel Institute of Technology and architect Charles M. Burns, Jr., who had planned the renovations of 1889, was hired to design a new church. The new building, of Italian Romanesque design, was ready for its first service on Palm Sunday, 1903, and it was consecrated in 1906 by Ozi Whitaker, Bishop of Pennsylvania.

Meanwhile, talk had begun about a cathedral in Philadelphia. Bishop Philip Rhinelander suggested building a cathedral in the early 1900s, but that plan never came about.[19] A cathedral chapter was formed in 1919 and a tract of land was purchased for what was to be a grand building, one of the size and scope of European cathedrals. Ground was broken in 1932, and construction began, but, because of lack of funds, only a chapel was completed and the project was abandoned. The chapel became known as St. Mary's at the Cathedral, and it houses a small congregation to this date.

Visitors to the cathedral probably will notice first the tower, a 130-foot-high square structure capped with a Romanesque-detailed balustrade and an octagonal lantern at the northwest corner of the building.

Inside, several architectural styles, from Byzantine to Renaissance to Norman, can be found. Most of the interior woodwork is of Flemish oak, including beams with carved angels. The dominant feature is the semi-dome mural above the chancel. The mural, painted by Edwin H. Blashfield, best known for his work on the great central dome in the Library of Congress in Washington, depicts a choir of angels.

Some unusual stained glass windows are found among the more than 40 in the cathedral. Of particular note are the 14 clerestory windows which tell the story of the episcopate in the Episcopal Church. The windows, from the Hardman Glass Company of England, include the seals of 14 dioceses.

Pittsburgh
Mid Atlantic

Trinity Cathedral has been a landmark in downtown Pittsburgh for more than 100 years, its spire soaring among office buildings.

Trinity has served Pittsburgh since 1761, when John Ormsby began reading Morning Prayer weekly at Fort Pitt for the citizens of the community. A priest was sent from Maryland during the Revolutionary War, and services were being held in private homes or the courthouse.[20]

In 1787, land was obtained for a church building, but it was 1805 before a building was completed. A brick, octagonal-shaped building, known as "The Round Church" was constructed and served the congregation for 20 years, when it became overcrowded and inadequate.

The consecration of the second Trinity Church was held June 12, 1825, by William White, first Bishop of Pennsylvania, on the site of the present cathedral. The building was described as a "standard protestant meeting house, but gothicized and improved."[21]

Pittsburgh experienced rapid growth in industry and population in the 1850s and 60s. The Diocese of Western Pennsylvania was created in 1865, and Trinity Parish began to plan for growth with another new building. The second Trinity was razed in 1869 to make room for a new edifice.

The present cathedral building was consecrated on St. Paul's Day, January 25, 1872, by Bishop John Kerfoot. The architectural style is 14th century early decorated, a form of English Gothic, and is executed in cut stone. It was designed by the rector at that time, James van Trump. The exterior of the building remains essentially the same today as when it was built.

Trinity became a cathedral on Trinity Sunday, June 3, 1928. The Diocese of Pittsburgh had been created in 1910 when Western Pennsylvania was split into two dioceses. Trinity's properties were transferred to the Chapter of Trinity Cathedral Church of the Diocese of Pittsburgh. The designation of cathedral status made official what had existed for more than 62 years—Trinity was the headquarters of the bishop.[22]

A destructive fire hit the cathedral the night of June 18, 1967, gutting the interior. Most furnishings, the organ, windows and the floor were destroyed by the fire, It was decided to rebuild, creating a more modern, contemporary cathedral while retaining the old dignity and grace.

The result of the rebuilding, which was completed in 1969, was considerable change in the interior. New windows were installed, the altar became freestanding, chancel space was increased, new lighting, audio system and air conditioning were installed, the 14-foot-high Heroic Cross was suspended above the altar, and the undercroft was developed.

The high altar is the focal point of the building. The plain steel table normally is adorned with a variety of embroidered coverings. The cathedra is carved in oak, with its canopy consisting of carved tracery and angels. The carved pulpit contains figures of saints, prophets and bishops.

Trinity's stained glass windows include some installed when the church was constructed, and others which were part of the rebuilding. The windows in the apse, transepts, west wall and clerestory date from 1872.

The eight windows in the nave were installed in 1968 and were made by the Hunt Stained Glass Studio of Pittsburgh. They depict Christ as Lord and Savior, Teacher, Healer, Worker, King, Prince of Peace, Judge, and Christ and the Family.

Mid America

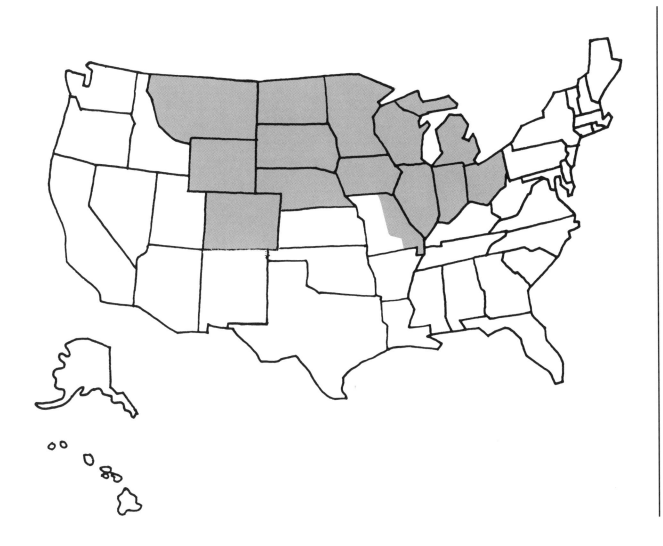

The Dioceses of

Minnesota
Chicago
Colorado
Eau Claire
Fond du Lac
Indianapolis
Iowa
Michigan
Milwaukee
Missouri
Montana
Nebraska
North Dakota
Northern Indiana
Ohio
Quincy
South Dakota
Southern Ohio
Springfield
Western Michigan
Wyoming

Minnesota

Mid America

The beautiful cathedral in Faribault has the distinction of being the first built as a cathedral in the Episcopal Church. It is unusual in that it is one of two cathedrals in the Diocese of Minnesota.

Our Merciful Saviour's history can be traced back to Trinity Sunday, June 3, 1855, when the first service was held in a home with three persons present. Thomas Wilcoxson walked 98 miles round trip to officiate.[1]

Bishop Jackson Kemper, whose missionary jurisdiction included Minnesota, assigned the Rev. James Lloyd Breck to work in Faribault out of the Associate Mission for Minnesota in St. Paul. In 1858, Breck outlined his plans at a meeting of citizens of Faribault. He envisioned a college for male students, a "seminary" for female students and a church to be located nearby. The educational institutions would be known as The Bishop Seabury University.[2]

A church was built by mid-summer of 1858 and was known as the Church of the Good Shepherd.

The designation of a cathedral had been mentioned by Breck in 1860.[3] When Bishop Henry B. Whipple laid the cornerstone July 16, 1862, the church was named the Cathedral of Our Merciful Saviour. The building was designed in plain Gothic style by James Renwick of Renwick and Company of New York City and was constructed of native blue limestone.

The first service in the new church was held on Whitsunday, May 16, 1869, even though the building was not completed. It was consecrated by Bishop Kemper on the Feast of St. John the Baptist, June 24, 1869. The cornerstone for a divinity school was laid the following day.

Bishop Samuel C. Edsall succeeded Whipple, and moved his headquarters to Minneapolis in 1902, but the Faribault church remained the cathedral. Our Merciful Saviour's handsome English perpendicular Gothic tower was designed by the firm of Cram, Goodhue and Ferguson. It was completed in 1902 and was dedicated in memory of Whipple.

The Seabury seminary merged with Western Seminary of Chicago in 1933, and became Seabury Western Seminary in Evanston, Illinois.

Meanwhile, additions and renovations in 1934 included the addition of a chapel and the installation of a new altar.

In 1941, the convention of the Diocese of Minnesota determined that St. Mark's, Minneapolis, should be the cathedral. On November 13, 1941, the chapter of the new cathedral issued a statement which read in part:

"The act by which St. Mark's becomes the Cathedral Church of Minnesota does not mean that we will abandon the cathedral in Faribault—the first cathedral built for this purpose on American soil. . . .It will remain as it was dedicated—. . . an historic and spiritual shrine."[4]

A memorable occasion for Our Merciful Saviour occurred August 7, 1954 when more than 450 delegates to the Anglican Congress in Minneapolis made a pilgrimage. The visitors included Archbishop of Canterbury Geoffrey Fisher and Presiding Bishop Henry Knox Sherrill.

The altar is Bedford stone. Its central panel is a bas-relief of da Vinci's Last Supper in Tennessee marble. The octagonal stone font is the cathedral's original. The elaborately-carved cathedra is possibly the oldest piece of furniture in the cathedral.[5] The pews also are the originals and are made of white pine from the woods of northern Minnesota.

All the stained glass windows were designed by the George Morgan Studio of New York City and installed in 1869.

Minnesota
Mid America

St. Mark's has the unusual distinction of being one of two cathedrals in the Diocese of Minnesota. The largest Episcopal church in Minnesota, it existed for 83 years before being designated a cathedral.

The congregation began in 1858, when a small mission chapel was organized in north Minneapolis. A wooden structure was built, then moved by ox sled to a new site downtown in 1863. The parish grew rapidly and needed a new building, which was constructed in 1870.

The present edifice was designed by Edwin H. Hewitt, a member of the parish, and was used for the first time in 1910. It was built in Gothic style with pointed arches and ribbing.

Minneapolis was the headquarters of the Bishop of Minnesota from 1902, when Bishop Samuel C. Edsall moved from Faribault, but the Cathedral of Our Merciful Saviour in Faribault remained the bishop's church until 1941, when diocesan convention determined that St. Mark's should become the cathedral.

On November 12, 1941, Bishop Frank A. McElwain accepted St. Mark's as the cathedral, although Our Merciful Saviour retained its cathedral status. When the constitution of the new corporation was adopted, it named the parish "The Cathedral Church of St. Mark," and it was to be "the diocesan church belonging to clergy and laity, the official and spiritual home of the bishop, and the center of diocesan work and worship."[6]

St. Mark's, like many cathedrals, is still being built. Stone capitals are being carved and new windows added.

The cathedral was the host for the first World Congress of the Anglican Communion in 1954. The event is commemorated by a seal in the floor in the crossing.

A person entering St. Mark's will encounter 26 bosses carved around the door. The bosses depict scenes and symbols of the life and history of Minnesota, including airplanes, teepees, grain elevators and gophers.

Upon entering the building, one is drawn to the high altar, made of a single block of Kasota stone. The reredos behind the altar has Christ as the central figure, surrounded by Moses and Elijah, the four gospel writers and other saints.

There are several interesting capital carvings in the choir area, including angels with various musical instruments, an illustration of the woman at the well, and a depiction of Peter's attempt to walk on water.

The pulpit, designed in the form of a chalice, has six well-known preachers carved in it. The lectern contains three figures from the Bible: Ezekiel, David and St. John. Next to the lectern is a sculpture of the Resurrection created by Minnesota sculptor Paul Granlund.

Two polychromed mahogany figures on both sides of the door leading into the narthex portray the young David confronting Goliath, and Youth seeking certainty and courage. They were created by sculptor John Rood, who also carved the facade, the west entrance and some of the capitals.

The west entrance, on the right side of the building, has exterior figures representing the five races of humanity. The link between the worldwide Anglican Communion and the Episcopal Church is shown in the carvings of Canterbury Cathedral and the church in Jamestown, Virginia.

The large window above the high altar illustrates the Ascension, with the ascending Christ the dominant figure, surrounded by angels, 11 apostles and 10 men and women significant in church history. A window above the pulpit depicts the church's patron saint, Mark.

Chicago
Mid America

The Cathedral of St. James is the second cathedral in the Diocese of Chicago, and is serving its second term as a "mother church."

The parish of St. James was organized in 1834 by eight trustees. There was enough growth to provide for the construction of a square, brick church building in 1837, which was used for the first time on Easter Day.

The congregation soon outgrew the little building and ground was broken for a second edifice on March 25, 1856. That church, constructed of Athens stone, seated more than 1,000 and was consecrated by Henry J. Whitehouse, Bishop of Illinois, May 19, 1864.

When the Great Chicago Fire struck the city in 1871, the majority of the families in the neighborhood around the church lost all of their possessions.[7] Only the tower and outer walls and foundation of the church building remained.

Construction of a new building began almost at once. The architectural firm of Clarke and Faulkner of Chicago was hired to design a new church. A temporary chapel was built to house the congregation during construction. Services began there April 28, 1872, and continued until November, 1873, when the basement of the new structure was finished.

The new church was designed in Gothic revival style, almost exactly like the one which was destroyed by fire. The first service was held in what is now the cathedral October 9, 1875.

Meanwhile, in the 1850s, Bishop Whitehouse had been attempting to secure land for the construction of a bishop's chapel, which would become, in his mind, a cathedral. He also planned for a cathedral in the English tradition.[8]

When that idea failed to develop, Bishop Whitehouse established a cathedral in the parish church of Sts. Peter and Paul March 17, 1861. It became the first cathedral in the Episcopal Church, and served as a cathedral for 60 years.[9]

In 1921, a fire destroyed the cathedral. That brought about more serious discussions about the cathedral concept in Chicago. Among the options being studied was the possibility of St. James' becoming the cathedral, a plan which had been raised as early as 1920.[10]

Some noted architects had submitted plans for a new, grand cathedral following the fire of 1921, but the decision eventually turned toward St. James'.

On June 4, 1928, members of St. James' parish voted to turn over their property to the bishop and cathedral chapter for the purpose of becoming a pro-cathedral.

Its life as a pro-cathedral was short. When George C. Stewart became the sixth bishop in 1930, he made the parish of which he had been rector, St. Luke's, Evanston, the pro-cathedral, and St. James' returned to parish status in 1931.

Wallace E. Conkling, seventh Bishop of Chicago, resurrected the idea of a new cathedral when he addressed diocesan convention in 1945. His plans for a large complex were not received favorably by the diocese.[11]

The next Bishop of Chicago, Gerald F. Burrill, believed the most realistic solution to establishing a permanent cathedral was to return to St. James', and it became the cathedral in 1955.

A major renovation of the church took place in 1962, and another renovation took place in 1984-85, when the cathedral was restored to its Victorian mode of 1888.

The cathedral's altar is of dark marble and was installed in 1962. The reredos predates an 1880 renovation.

The nave windows are of painted glass and date from the late 1880s. They depict a variety of biblical scenes.

Colorado
Mid America

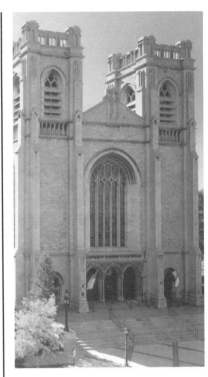

Denver's beautiful cathedral is the home of a large, active congregation and the center of several significant ministries which serve both the diocese and the city.

The cathedral's foundation was the organizing of the parish of St. John's in the Wilderness on January 23, 1860. Six days later, the Rev. John H. Kehler, newly arrived from Maryland by stagecoach, held the first service in a log building. Joseph Talbot, Missionary Bishop of the Northwest, visited the congregation in November, 1861, and soon after that St. John's was incorporated by the first Legislative Assembly of Colorado Territory.

On July 20, 1862, Bishop Talbot returned to dedicate the congregation's first building, a small brick edifice which had been built by Southern Methodists in 1859 and had been the first church building in Denver. A wooden addition was made the following year.

The idea of a cathedral for Colorado was discussed soon after the arrival of John F. Spalding as Missionary Bishop of Colorado in 1873, but it was some time before the bishop could carry out his plan.

When H. Martyn Hart was called to Denver in 1879 as rector of St. John's, the cathedral plan began to take shape. Hart was an Englishman, moving to Denver from Blackheath, and within a month following his arrival, Bishop Spalding appointed him dean of a proposed cathedral. On October 2 of that year, Bishop Spalding announced plans for a new church which would be the cathedral of the Diocese of Colorado.

The cathedral building was completed in 1881, and the first service was held November 1, the Feast of All Saints. The building was of Victorian Romanesque design and served Denver until May 15, 1903, when an arsonist destroyed it. Most of the windows and carvings were saved.

Plans to rebuild were made immediately. A new piece of land was purchased, and a national competition for plans for the cathedral was held. The firm of Tracy and Swartwout of New York City was chosen.

A Chapter House was built in 1904 and used for services until the new building was ready in 1911. The first service was held that year on November 5. The building, which is the present cathedral, was of English Gothic design constructed of Indiana limestone. It is one of the larger Episcopal cathedrals, with a nave 183 feet long and 65 feet high, seating more than 1,000. St. John's was consecrated on the Feast of St. Barnabas, June 11, 1925, by Bishop Irving Peake Johnson as St. John's Church in the Wilderness. By a strange quirk, the cathedral, whose cornerstone had been laid in expectation that the name would be the Cathedral of St. John the Evangelist, was dedicated to St. John the Baptist.[12]

Many of the cathedral's finest appointments are near the altar. The altar screen and altar, saved from the fire in the first cathedral, were carved by Josef Mayr and Peter Rendl of Oberammergau. The work of the same carvers can be seen in the 17 free-standing figures in the reredos.

The canopied choir and clergy stalls have carvings of small animals and plants of Colorado, and were added during a refurbishing in 1943. The handsome cathedra was executed in 1918 by Lamb and Company of New York City.

There are 51 stained glass windows in the cathedral, 13 of which were saved from the fire. Some of the most striking are the seven apse windows designed by Charles J. Connick of Boston. They show the Ascension of Christ, with his earthly companions in the side panels.

The large window over the portal depicts the last judgment and was designed by Edward Frampton of London.

Eau Claire
Mid America

Christ Church Cathedral serves one of the smallest dioceses (in membership) of the Episcopal Church. The diocese comprises the northwest part of Wisconsin and is one of three in the state.

Services were held in various locations in Eau Claire as early as 1858 by a deacon, Abraham Peabody. When Jackson Kemper, Bishop of Wisconsin, visited Eau Claire in July, 1861, it marked the last record of any activity of the Episcopal Church there until the close of the Civil War.[13]

On June 24, 1866, the Rev. Charles J. Hendley established a mission in Eau Claire. It was formally organized in 1870. Services were held in local halls, one of which burned in 1871, destroying records of the early years of Christ Church.

Two years later, on September 10, 1873, the cornerstone was laid for the congregation's first church by William E. Armitage of Wisconsin in what was his last act as bishop before his death. The new building, an English Gothic frame structure with a spire and bell, was completed in 1875.

Christ Church became a parish in 1881, and the congregation grew steadily. In 1909, work began on a new parish house, which was patterned after Benham Abbey in Norfolkshire, England, and on a new chancel. That area, designed by the firm of Purcell, Feick and Elmslie of Minneapolis on a modified Gothic plan, was opened December 21, 1910.

The last service in the old church was held Easter Day, 1910. The building was taken down in sections and moved to Owen, Wisconsin, in 1915, where it was rebuilt as St. Katherine's Mission.

The next step in expansion was to build the nave of the new church. On August 21, 1915, Reginald H. Weller, Bishop of Fond du Lac, a former rector of Christ Church, laid the cornerstone for the new building. The new structure was opened April 2, 1916, and consecrated in 1920 by the Rt. Rev. Walter W. Webb of Milwaukee, even though the interior of the church was far from complete.

In 1928, the Diocese of Eau Claire was created out of the Diocese of Milwaukee, and Christ Church offered itself as the pro-cathedral until such time as a permanent cathedral could be erected.[14] Frank Wilson, rector of Christ Church, was elected first Bishop of Eau Claire, and established his parish as a pro-cathedral in 1929, and as the cathedral in 1931.

The focal point of the interior is the altar with its reredos. Both are made of Carrara marble and were installed in 1910 when the chancel was completed.

The bishop's throne and accompanying stalls were dedicated in 1927 and include the seal of the diocese below the canopy. The rood beam, surmounted by the figure of Christ the King on the cross, was dedicated in 1927 and executed by the Langs of Oberammergau, as was the carving of the Last Supper near the entrance to the chapel. The pulpit, lectern and rail were dedicated on Christmas Eve, 1924.

Many fine examples of stained glass windows are found in the cathedral. The earlier windows were designed and executed by the firm of Heaton, Butler and Bayne of London. The remaining windows were created by the Wippell Company of Exeter, England in 1951.[15]

The window above the high altar depicts the Resurrection and was installed at the same time as the altar and reredos. The shields on each side of the window are those of the 12 apostles. The Nativity window, at the other end of the church, was given in 1916 when the nave was completed. Between those two windows are eight large ones which illustrate aspects of Christ's ministry on earth.

Fond du Lac
Mid America

Fond du Lac's lovely cathedral contains some of the finest examples of religious wood carving in the United States. Fond du Lac, which covers the northeastern portion of Wisconsin, has been a center of the catholic revival in the Episcopal Church.

Episcopal services were held in Fond du Lac as early as 1842. Jackson Kemper, Missionary Bishop of the Northwest, led worship in the home of Governor Tallmadge in 1845, and services were held on a fairly regular basis beginning in 1849.[16]

The congregation erected a small, frame church which was consecrated by Bishop Kemper July 8, 1852. St. Paul's soon outgrew its facility and a larger, stone church was built on the site of the present cathedral, opening December 25, 1866.

The Diocese of Fond du Lac was created out of the Diocese of Wisconsin October 29, 1874, and John Henry Hobart Brown became its first bishop in 1876. St. Paul's congregation voted to turn over the church to Bishop Brown as the cathedral of the new diocese.

Much of the cathedral was destroyed by fire January 25, 1884, the Feast of St. Paul. The sexton had built "heavy fires in both furnaces about 2 o'clock in the morning to get the building warm for services."[17] Only the tower and the outer wall remained.

Services were held in a cathedral school building for the next three years, until the cathedral could be rebuilt. The cornerstone for the new church was laid October 28, 1884. The first service in the present building was held Easter Day, 1887. The new Gothic revival stone church was larger than its predecessor, with transepts and a chancel added.

When Charles C. Grafton, second Bishop of Fond du Lac, called for election of a bishop coadjutor, it led to an event which caused an uproar throughout the Episcopal Church. Reginald Weller was consecrated November 8, 1900, at St. Paul's in the first consecration in the history of the American church to use full catholic ceremonial. A picture of bishops present in copes and mitres received national publicity.[18]

Many interesting appointments are found inside St. Paul's. The baptismal font, near the main entrance, is a bowl of Italian marble on a pedestal of Tennessee marble under a canopy. On the other side of the entrance is the Shrine of St. Margaret. The statue was a gift of an English noblewoman and appeared at the French International Exposition in 1894, winning a first prize in sculpture.[19]

A dominant feature of the nave is the wood carvings. Statues of the 12 Apostles line the walls, and angels are carved at the ends of the hammer beams in the ceiling. A statue of St. Paul is found near the entrance. All of the carvings were done at Oberammergau in the 1890s.

The stone pulpit was put in place in 1889 and is a gift from the Church of the Advent, Boston, where Bishop Grafton had been rector. The figure of St. Augustine is believed to be a likeness of Bishop Brown.[20]

More wood carvings are found on the rood beam, including the unusual figures of the Angel of Life and the Angel of Death in the pedestals of the rood.

The reredos behind the altar has three carved panels, two of them showing events in the life of St. Paul, and the central panel illustrating the Ascension.

Among the interesting windows in St. Paul's are those above the main entrance, with scenes from the Old Testament. King David is in the center flanked by Aaron and Isaiah. Windows in the nave show scenes from the life of St. Paul. There is a rose window in each transept.

Indianapolis
Mid America

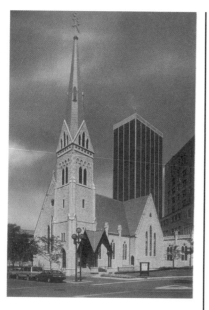

Christ Church Cathedral has been located on Monument Circle in downtown Indianapolis for more than 150 years—all its life.

Jackson Kemper, the Episcopal Church's first missionary bishop, who was a key figure in the founding of many American cathedrals, visited Indianapolis for the first time in 1835. A year later, he began to solicit funds for building an Episcopal church.

The first service was held July 9, 1837, by the Rev. J. B. Britton, and the parish was organized officially four days later. The cornerstone for the first building was laid by Bishop Kemper May 7, 1838, the same year the Diocese of Indianapolis was formed. The first service in the new building was held November 18, 1838, and it was consecrated a month later by Bishop Kemper.

By 1856, a new building was needed. Irish architect William Tinsley was selected to design it, and the cornerstone was laid June 25, 1857. The original frame church was sold and moved, and the congregation worshiped in the House of Representatives and Temperance Hall while construction took place.[21]

The first service in the new church, which is the present cathedral, was held May 29, 1859. The exterior of the building has changed little since that time. Tinsley's design was of early Gothic revival style and was constructed of Indiana limestone.

Finishing touches were needed to complete the building. A set of bells was installed in the tower in 1860. A gallery was built on the west wall for the choir and organ in 1866. Sunday school students donated a cathedra for the bishop that year, even though Christ Church had not achieved cathedral status. The spire was completed in 1869, and a new episcopal residence was constructed in 1871.

By 1882, Indianapolis had six Episcopal churches and St. Paul's was the pro-cathedral. The following year, Grace Church replaced St. Paul's as the pro-cathedral.[22]

A parish house was constructed and a wooden porch was added to Christ Church building in 1900 and many interior improvements were made, including the installation of Tiffany-style stained glass windows.

Major renovations, especially in the sanctuary, took place in 1954 at a cost of nearly $300,000. Another major event took place that year when Christ Church was instituted as the cathedral of the diocese.

Further improvements were made in 1973, when the nave and sanctuary were repainted, pews refinished, a carpet and sound system installed, light fixtures rebuilt, bells in the tower restored and the parish hall refurbished. Stained glass windows were restored in 1979. The nave and parish house were renovated in 1983.

Among the furnishings of the cathedral is a baptismal font designed by the renowned Ralph Adams Cram of Boston. The figure atop the font was sculpted by John Angel, the English creator of sculpture for the Cathedral of St. John the Divine in New York City.

The white marble high altar was elevated during the renovation of 1954. The grillwork at the pulpit is of bronze.

There are some good examples of stained glass in the cathedral. The north transept lancet windows were designed by Steven Bridges and depict the history of the Anglican Church and Christ Church. They were installed during the 1953-54 renovation. The Tiffany-style memorial windows in the nave, west end and south transept date back to 1900. Some of them were executed by the Tiffany Company.

Iowa
Mid America

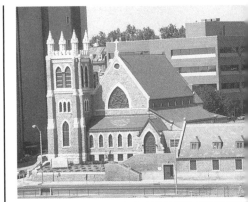

When C. Christopher Epting, Bishop of Iowa, designated St. Paul's Church the cathedral for the Diocese of Iowa, it became the third American diocese to have two cathedrals. St. Paul's was established as the cathedral by vote of diocesan convention November 7, 1992, and joined Trinity Cathedral, Davenport, as Iowa's two "bishop's churches."

The action meant St. Paul's became the episcopal and liturgical center of the diocese, leaving Trinity with its title and a new role as a mission center for eastern Iowa. The move was made because the bishop's office and his cathedral were separated by nearly 200 miles. The bishop's office was moved from Davenport to Des Moines during World War II.

St. Paul's was established October 15, 1854, when a small group met for services at a local Presbyterian church, with the Rev. Everett W. Peet of Rahway, New Jersey, officiating. A meeting was held that day to organize a parish and the name St. Paul's was chosen.[23] Later, services were held in the Polk County courthouse.

In 1856, a new church was constructed. The brick and frame building was consecrated by Bishop Henry W. Lee in July, 1857, but it wasn't long before a larger structure was needed. Two lots were purchased in 1870, and in 1884 construction began on the present St. Paul's building. The architectural firm of Foster and Liebbe designed the new church, adapting English cathedral Gothic with simplified rural Gothic. It was dedicated April 5, 1885, by Bishop William S. Perry.

Restoration projects took place in 1937, 1949, 1968 and 1987, with the 1987 work the most significant.

A visitor to St. Paul's enters through the narthex under a large window which shows the parish's patron, St. Paul, preaching while holding a scroll in his hand. The window was crafted by the Wippell-Mowbray Studio of Exeter,

—*Trinity Cathedral, Davenport*

England. At the top of the stairs leading to the nave are windows showing Paul, St. Mary, Christ the Good Shepherd, St. Elizabeth, St. Peter and Christ the King.

Inside, the six windows along both walls of the nave show various Christian symbols. The large rose window above the center entrance from the narthex to the nave has a figure of Christ in the center and has a diameter of 14 feet. Many of the windows were damaged seriously, particularly the rose window, in 1970 when a bomb exploded across the street in the office of the Chamber of Commerce.

The circular apse at the end of the building is a departure from Gothic style, which usually has a square or rectangular termination. The reredos was installed in 1937, and three windows located there were moved to the narthex. Those three windows and the four which remain behind the altar, depicting the four evangelists, Matthew, Mark, Luke and John, are the oldest in the building. The area in the apse and choir was paneled in wainscoting during the 1937 renovation.

Trinity Cathedral, Davenport, one of the nations oldest, is the result of the merging of three parishes: Trinity Church, St. Luke's, and Christ Church. Begun in 1867, the building was dedicated in 1873 by Henry W. Lee, the bishop whose vision led to the cathedral's construction.

Trinity is of Gothic design, more reminiscent of English Gothic style than European, especially in its rounded apse. The exterior was built of Iowa limestone and trimmed with Indiana limestone. The interior also has a Gothic look with its intricate beaming. A small carved stone in the wall behind the lectern was sent to Trinity by the dean and chapter of Westminster Abbey, where it stood for centuries in "the Statesman's Corner." The pews, donated by Bishop Lee, are black walnut made from native Iowa wood.

Michigan
Mid America

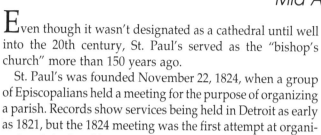

Even though it wasn't designated as a cathedral until well into the 20th century, St. Paul's served as the "bishop's church" more than 150 years ago.

St. Paul's was founded November 22, 1824, when a group of Episcopalians held a meeting for the purpose of organizing a parish. Records show services being held in Detroit as early as 1821, but the 1824 meeting was the first attempt at organization. It is the oldest Episcopal parish in Michigan and the upper Midwest.[24]

John Henry Hobart, Bishop of New York, visited the congregation in 1827 and laid the cornerstone for its first church building. He returned the following year to consecrate the new church, made of brick and wood and Gothic in style. That building was enlarged twice.

Meetings were held beginning in 1832 to form a Diocese of Michigan. In 1836, Samuel A. McCoskry was elected Bishop of Michigan and later was elected rector of St. Paul's. He was rector for 27 years and bishop for 46 years. While Bishop McCoskry held both roles, St. Paul's functioned as the bishop's church.[25]

In 1850, the church and land were sold and the money reinvested in a new lot. Construction began on a new church, and the congregation held services at nearby Firemen's Hall from after Easter Day, 1852, until its new building could be used. It was dedicated in December of that year.

When industrial development and new railroad lines transformed the neighborhood where St. Paul's was located, it was decided toward the end of the century to move the location of the parish. The site of the present building was purchased in 1892, and four years later a parish house and a chapel, to serve as a temporary church, were opened.

Bishop Charles Williams, who was consecrated in 1906, accepted an invitation from St. Paul's offering use of the church as a cathedral. The cornerstone for the new cathedral was laid in 1908.

The building was designed by Ralph Adams Cram in 13th century English Gothic style, and was completed and dedicated in 1911. It was consecrated in 1919.

On Palm Sunday, 1922, the cathedral's 11 a.m. service was broadcast by radio, and with the exception of a few summer Sundays in the early 1920s, it has been broadcast weekly ever since. It is the oldest religious program broadcast by radio in the country.[26]

The cathedral is unfinished according to Cram's plan, as the tower never was completed.

Inside, the focal point is the high altar, made of Caen stone. An altar stone from Canterbury Cathedral is set into the top of the altar. The reredos includes seven figures carved by Kirchnayer of Oberammergau.

Among the stained glass windows at St. Paul's is the large east window over the high altar, which depicts the Passion, Resurrection and Ascension. The 12 windows in the sanctuary, six on each side, are of 15th century glass and are known as the Spanish windows because they came to Detroit from a Spanish cathedral. In the nave, the three windows on the north side represent the Revelation of St. John and on the south side, miracles and parables. Over the west gallery is a rose window of the four evangelists.

Nativity Chapel, in the south transept, has some interesting appointments. A 15th century Flemish oak carving showing Jesus in prayer in Gethsemane is found on the pillar. Ten carved and polychromed scenes from the life of Joseph of the Old Testament are found on the altar rail.

Milwaukee
Mid America

The brick building near Milwaukee's lakefront which once served as a Congregational church has a long, interesting history as a center of Episcopal ministry in Wisconsin.

Initial steps toward the creation of a cathedral were taken during the episcopate of Jackson Kemper, who became Bishop of Wisconsin in 1859. In his address to the 1866 Diocesan Council, he urged development of a cathedral. That same council elected a suffragan bishop, William E. Armitage, to whom Bishop Kemper gave the duty of developing a cathedral in Milwaukee.[27]

Soon after Bishop Armitage arrived in 1867, Trinity Church in Milwaukee, already a union of two parishes, deeded to the diocese all its assets and property. A month after Trinity was closed, Bishop Kemper reopened it as All Saints' parish and made it the pro-cathedral of the diocese.[28]

All Saints' congregation purchased some lots July 1, 1869, and Bishop Kemper laid the cornerstone for a new cathedral on the Feast of All Saints, November 1, 1869. Bishop Kemper died the following year and was succeeded by Bishop Armitage. Meanwhile, financial problems caused construction on the cathedral to be halted after only the basement had been completed. In 1870, the property was abandoned to its mortgager.

Other lots were purchased by the congregation in 1871, and the former chapel of Trinity Church was moved to this new location. In 1872, neighboring Olivet Congregational Church moved into its new building, which had been under construction since 1868, and ran into dissension and financial problems. On June 1 of that year, Bishop Armitage acquired the title to that edifice, and the following year Diocesan Council accepted the church as a cathedral. Bishop Armitage died in December, 1873, and, for a time, the cathedral plan was put aside. Finally in 1882, the cathedral came into being.

The Diocese of Wisconsin became the Diocese of Milwaukee in 1886. The pro-cathedral was consecrated as the cathedral November 1, 1898, by Bishop Isaac Nicholson.

The design of the cathedral is credited to Edward Townsend Mix of Milwaukee. The walls are of cream-colored pressed brick trimmed with limestone. A 190-foot octagonal spire with a pyramid point is the dominant feature of the exterior.

All Saints' was a pioneer in Anglo-Catholic liturgical expression. The Eucharist has been celebrated daily since 1879, the sacrament has been reserved since 1895, and incense was in use as early as 1902.[29]

The interior is dominated by the altar with its reredos and triptych, designed by Eugene W. Mason of New York City. The gold-hued Sienna marble altar and Italian renaissance triptych were installed in 1919. The seven brass hanging lamps symbolize the seven-fold gifts of the Holy Spirit.

Some fine wood carving is found in All Saints', including the oak cathedra, which was installed in 1910 and rebuilt in 1944. Another bishop's throne is found outside the chancel area near the font. It is said to have been used by the first Presiding Bishop of the Episcopal Church, William White, in the late 1700s.

The windows in the sanctuary were made by the English firm of Heaton, Butler and Bayne, and were installed in 1908. The large rondel window in the gallery was made by the same firm in 1909 and depicts Christ the King. Windows in the side aisles and in the narthex (with one exception) were executed by Lavers and Westlake of England and were installed between 1892 and 1899.

Missouri
Mid America

Christ Church Cathedral, St. Louis

Christ Church was the first Episcopal congregation west of the Mississippi River. It was founded November 1, 1819, the Feast of All Saints, when 46 persons committed themselves to giving and drew up articles of organization. The first Episcopal service had been held three days earlier by the Rev. John Ward, who had arrived from Lexington, Kentucky.[30]

The parish became disorganized in 1824, and regular services were not held again until the following year. Services were held then in nearby protestant churches. In 1826, land was purchased and construction began on a church building. That edifice was completed November 10, 1829 and was consecrated May 25, 1834, by Benjamin B. Smith, first Bishop of Kentucky.

When Jackson Kemper was consecrated Missionary Bishop of Missouri and Indiana in 1835 he made St. Louis the center of his ministry. He served as rector of Christ Church until 1840. The congregation grew rapidly and soon outgrew its church. Construction began in 1836 for a second building, which was consecrated February 17, 1839 by Bishop Kemper.

Only 16 years later, the vestry began to plan for another new building. In 1859, several noted architects were invited to submit plans for a new church.[31] The firm of Leopold Eidlitz of New York City was chosen to design the present building. The design was from 14th century English Gothic style, cruciform in shape. The cornerstone was laid by Bishop Cicero Hawks April 22, 1860, but construction was delayed by the Civil War.

The congregation was able to use the chapel of the new building in April, 1862, but the first service in the nave wasn't held until Christmas Day, 1867. At that time it lacked the intended flying buttresses, narthex and bell tower.

In 1888 Bishop Daniel Tuttle designated Christ Church the cathedral for the Diocese of Missouri. He consecrated it in 1890.

Some notable additions were made to the cathedral early in the 20th century. The altar and reredos were dedicated on Christmas Day, 1911, and the bell tower and narthex on Easter Day, 1912. The cathedra was installed in 1916.

Another renovation took place in 1991 when the wall and arch at the southwest corner of the church was restored. Built in 1895, they were removed in 1988 because of deterioration.

The reredos is the crowning glory of this cathedral. The altar and reredos were sculpted of Caen stone from Normandy, France, by Harry Hems of Exeter, England. The reredos is 35 feet high, 28 feet wide, and contains 52 carved figures. It is similar to altar screens in the English cathedrals at Winchester and St. Albans. Because of this similarity, a stone from each cathedral is set into the fabric of the St. Louis building. The stone from Winchester is set in the east wall of the north transept, and the St. Albans stone is on the left of the center door leading from the nave to the narthex.

The reredos figures include the crucified Christ in the center with the attendant figures of the Blessed Virgin and John the Beloved Disciple on each side.

The high altar is a single slab of Italian marble from Carrara. The large panel above the altar is a carving of the Nativity. Carved into the front of the altar are the Presentation, Resurrection and Annunciation.

The west windows of the nave were designed in 1896 by Englishman Charles Kempe and illustrate 11 scenes from the life of Christ. The Tiffany windows at the rear of the north aisle were installed in 1917 and represent hope and faith.

Montana

Mid America

Like many of the Episcopal Church's ministry efforts in the Northwest, St. Peter's owes its founding to Bishop Daniel Tuttle.

St. Peter's Mission was founded by Bishop Tuttle, first Bishop of Montana, in 1867. Mining had brought people from many parts of the country to Helena, and when Bishop Tuttle arrived, August 6, 1867, he noted in his memoirs that Helena was a "town of 4,000 inhabitants pitched in the bottom of a dirty mining gulch."[32]

The first Episcopal service in Helena was held five days after Bishop Tuttle's arrival by the bishop and his brother-in-law, the Rev. Edward N. Goddard. A meeting was held the following day with persons who were interested in forming a mission. Some of them were Presbyterians who had no church of their own.[33]

On December 19, 1868, Bishop Tuttle moved from Virginia City to Helena, took charge of the mission, and remained there for seven months.

The mission was vacant from 1870-1875, with occasional services conducted by either Bishop Tuttle or Mr. Goddard. Regular services resumed after that, and growth was noted. St. Peter's was organized as a parish August 27, 1879, and plans were made for a church. It was built at a cost of $12,000, and the first service was held October 19, 1879. The church was consecrated November 11, 1881.

Various forms of outreach followed. St. Peter's Hospital was established in 1883, a Chinese mission was organized in 1890 to teach English to the Chinese immigrants, and a parish school was organized around the turn of the century.

St. Peter's congregation eventually outgrew its little church, and Harold C. Whitehouse of Spokane, Washington, was hired to design a new building. Whitehouse had made a study of Anglican churches in England, and also designed the cathedral in Spokane. A foundation stone for the new building was laid by Bishop William F. Faber September 10, 1931. The last service in the old church was held in January, 1932, and the parish house of the new complex was available for a service February 7, 1932.

The new church was dedicated March 7, 1932, by Bishop Faber as the pro-cathedral of the diocese. It was constructed of modified Gothic design, built of stone. The pews and organ from the old church were moved into the new building.

A deanery building was constructed in 1941, and the cathedral was consecrated Thanksgiving Day, November 19, 1944. A new organ was dedicated in 1952, new pews were installed in 1955, and an educational building was completed in 1959. Renovation was made in 1967, when St. Peter's observed its centennial. Five years later, the pro-cathedral was designated the cathedral.

St. Peter's has excellent stained glass windows executed by Charles J. Connick Associates of Boston. The small window above the altar portrays St. Peter seated and holding a symbolic copy of St. Mark's Gospel. The nave window nearest the chapel depicts Bishop Tuttle and pioneer Christianity. Among the windows on the other side of the nave is one of the Virgin Mary, and another showing St. Paul. The window on the stair landing on the east side is believed to be from the Tiffany Studio.

The altar includes end panels carved with pine and bitter-root, native to Montana. The medallions on each end of the altar are of grapes and wheat, symbols of the Eucharist.

The rood beam cross is made of myrtle wood from Myrtle Point, near Marshfield, Oregon, believed to be the only place in this country where myrtle wood is found.

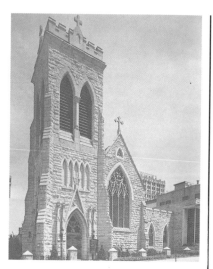

Trinity Cathedral, Omaha

Nebraska
Mid America

Nebraska's cathedral is one of the few in the Episcopal Church to be able to celebrate 100 years as a cathedral. Trinity observed its centennial in 1986. It had been a parish for 30 years before it became a cathedral.

A meeting was held April 17, 1856, to discuss the possibility of organizing a parish in Omaha. The first service was held three days later by the Rev. Edward Peet. In July of that year, Jackson Kemper, the Episcopal Church's first missionary bishop, and Bishop Henry W. Lee of Iowa held a service in the territorial legislative house in Omaha.

Trinity was organized later in 1856, and was attached to the Diocese of Iowa. A small church was erected in 1859 and served the parish for many years. The parish was incorporated April 21, 1862. At that time, the Missionary District of the Northwest was divided into three parts. The Nebraska headquarters were moved to Omaha in 1865 with the arrival of Bishop Robert H. Clarkson. Plans were made in 1867 for a new church, and that larger building was occupied in 1868. On March 4, 1868, Trinity became a pro-cathedral.

On November 10, 1869, the new church was destroyed by fire, and a temporary building was erected to house the congregation until a permanent structure could be built.

Even though there was only a temporary building in use, Bishop Clarkson advanced his plan for the establishment of a permanent cathedral in September, 1872.[34] The Diocesan Council approved, and Trinity was made the cathedral.

It took several years before construction could begin on a new cathedral. H.G. Harrison of New York City was selected as the architect, and construction began in 1880. The temporary building was moved off the property and placed in the middle of Capitol Avenue, to allow construction to begin on the same site. This "Church in the Middle of the Street" was used until 1981 when it was moved again.[35] It became known as St. Philip's Chapel.

Ground was broken for the new building May 15, 1880, and the cornerstone was laid 10 days later. The present Gothic cathedral building was completed in 1883 of blue limestone from Illinois and consecrated November 15 of that year.

Nativity Chapel was dedicated December 18, 1947. Exterior renovation was done in 1950 and more interior work was done the following spring.

All of Trinity's stained glass windows were installed when the cathedral was constructed. The large west window honors Bishop Kemper. There are 30 clerestory windows—16 on the south side and 14 on the north. They represent churches and institutions in Nebraska which were active when the cathedral was constructed. The apse contains 13 windows, with Christ in the center and six saints on each side. The large north window is in memory of George Selwyn, Bishop of New Zealand.

Trinity's altar has three panels filled with bronze reliefs which depict the Annunciation, Crucifixion and Ascension.

In 1991, it became necessary to close the nave and sanctuary when termites were discovered in much of the building. Pews and other furnishings were placed in storage and services were moved to the parish house while restoration took place. The discovery of the insects took place only a few years after a colony of 50,000 bees was found above the ceiling.[36]

The Diocese of Nebraska has another building which has served as a cathedral. St. Mark's Pro-Cathedral in Hastings, a Gothic building designed by Ralph Adams Cram, was the cathedral for the Missionary District of Western Nebraska, which became part of the Diocese of Nebraska.[37] Its first service was held in 1929.

North Dakota
Mid America

Gethsemane Cathedral, Fargo

North Dakota can claim the newest building among Episcopal cathedrals following a fire which destroyed an 89-year-old building September 12, 1989. For a time following the fire, services were held in a temporary location which Frank Clark, dean, called "a storefront church."

Gethsemane is believed to be the oldest house of worship in North Dakota, with the possible exception of a Roman Catholic chapel near Pembina. The first Episcopal service in Fargo was held August 29, 1872, by the Rev. J.F. Gillfillian of Brainerd, Minnesota. A mission was organized in 1873 by Bishop Robert H. Clarkson. A Rev. Mr. Henry held services in a tent, then in a small hall. That mission became known as the Church at the Crossing.[38]

A church was erected in 1874, but the building was not completed. A rectory was built the following year. The mission achieved parish status in 1877 and was known as Christ Church for the first two years of its existence. It was called Gethsemane beginning in 1879.[39]

The Missionary District of North Dakota was formed in 1883, and W.D. Walker, elected the first bishop, chose Fargo as his see city.

Bishop Walker soon began a novel form of ministry. He ordered a railroad car from the Pullman Company which became known as the Gospel Car. It provided seating for 80 and contained a font and pulpit.[40] Because of the large size of the district and the small number of churches, the car was taken by rail to the people of North Dakota.

The railroad car was called the Church of the Advent, its name in capital letters near the top of the car; painted on the side was "The Cathedral Car of North Dakota."[41]

A building which served until the fire was erected in 1899-1900. George Hancock, a Gethsemane parishioner, was the architect, and designed a Gothic revival form church. The building had wooden buttresses on a stone foundation with gabled transepts in a cruciform plan.

The first service was held February 11, 1900, with the dedication by Walker and Samuel Edsall, first Bishop of the State of North Dakota.

Bishop Edsall took temporary charge of the parish in May, 1900, and plans were soon formed to change the church from parochial to cathedral status. Gethsemane was designated the cathedral in September, 1900. The building was consecrated in December, 1913, by Bishop Cameron Mann.

The fire which struck in 1989 was believed to have been started by a propane torch being used to remove old paint from the exterior siding. The work was part of a $100,000 five-year improvement project begun that year. The bishop's throne and high altar were spared from the fire along with the communion vessels. Brass items are being repaired and refinished. Damage was estimated to be about $2 million, and included the pipe organ, vestments and more than half of the stained glass windows.

In November, 1990, Gethsemane's chapter voted to sell its property and to build a new church on a site purchased from the Roman Catholic Diocese of Fargo, about a mile away from the former cathedral. Architect Charles Moore of Austin, Texas, was contracted to design a new cathedral.[42] Ground breaking for the new building was held May 18, 1991. The exterior materials are board and batten wood cladding over masonry block walls, with some wood frame construction.[43] The new cathedral was in use for the first time at the diocesan convention in November, 1992, even though it was not completed.

Cathedral of St. James, South Bend

Northern Indiana
Mid America

It took more than a quarter of a century for the Episcopal Church to establish firm roots in South Bend. Episcopal services were held there as early as 1840, when worship was held in a Presbyterian church,[44] but there was no effort made to organize a parish until 1867.

Those first services were held shortly after the formation of the Diocese of Indiana, in 1838. Two years later, that diocese was added to the territory of Missionary Bishop Jackson Kemper, who was active all over the Midwest. In 1867, initial services were held in a local hall on Sunday afternoons; in November of that year, they were moved to a Dutch Reformed church, with clergy from nearby communities in charge.

A committee was formed December 15, 1867 to act as an informal vestry. The name St. James was chosen three days later. On July 6, 1868, a committee petitioned the Bishop of Indiana for organization of a church. Permission was granted three days later, and the first vestry was elected July 28, 1868.

Services were held infrequently from 1868 until 1871. A small, frame Gothic-style building was completed August 30, 1869, and the parish called its first rector and reorganized itself in 1871. The need for a larger building became obvious in 1872, and a lot was purchased. A small house on that lot became a rectory, and the little church was moved to the new lot and rebuilt. The church reopened February 20, 1873, but the congregation went through financial difficulties and considerable turnover in clergy for the next few years.

By the 1890s, growth and stability were noted, and the vestry decided in 1892 to build a new church. Ground was broken for the present building June 1, 1894, and the cornerstone was laid on the Feast of St. James, July 25, 1894. The first service in the new brick building was at midnight on Christmas Eve, 1894.

Many of the appointments now in use were given as memorials around the turn of the century. The undercroft, known as Cathedral Hall, was completed in 1929. The Bishop White Chapel, later known as the Chapel of the Holy Angels, was remodeled, along with the baptistry, in 1944. A major renovation took place in 1964, and additional properties were purchased in 1955 and 1962.

The Diocese of Northern Indiana was created in 1898 and consisted of 31 counties in the upper one-third of the state. It was called the Diocese of Michigan City, after its original see city, but the name was changed in 1919. St. James' was designated as the cathedral by the Rt. Rev. Reginald Mallett and consecrated in 1957. Previously, St. Paul's in nearby Mishawaka had served as the cathedral for a time.

St. James' contains some stained glass windows of note, particularly a rose window over the entrance made by the Tiffany Studio of New York, which had been exhibited at the Chicago World Fair in 1893. The sanctuary window is a memorial to the first three bishops of Indiana, and contains a figure of St. James in its center panel. Other windows were made by the Miles Studio and the McCully Studio, both of Chicago.

Ohio
Mid America

Trinity Cathedral is a splendid example of perpendicular Gothic architecture. The building is dominated by its massive square tower, which rises 108 feet above floor level.

Trinity was the first religious organization in Cleveland, beginning November 9, 1816 with a small gathering in a house. It was incorporated in 1828, eight years before Cleveland became a city. The present cathedral is the second to be called Trinity. The first building was used until early in the 20th century.

In 1890, the vestry of Trinity Church presented the building to William A. Leonard, Bishop of Ohio, to be the cathedral of the diocese. Not long afterward, work began on a new cathedral complex. Cathedral House, at the east end of the current building, was built by the end of the 19th century; then, on August 5, 1901, ground-breaking was held for the new cathedral. The last service in old Trinity was held June 29, 1902, and services were moved to the hall until September 29, 1907, when the new cathedral, designed by William Swinefurth, was consecrated in a service attended by about 2,000 people.[45]

The cathedral's exterior and interior are constructed mainly of Indiana limestone, with various types of marble used for the flooring.

One of Trinity's most interesting features is its baptistry. The font is made of white marble and contains stones from the River Jordan near the Damascus Ford where Jesus was baptized. The cover of the font is carved in oak and is a scale model of the tower of the cathedral. The carving above the baptistry altar dates from the 16th century and is from the area near Troyes, France. It once was a fragment of a choir screen.

The intricately-carved pulpit and base of the rood screen are constructed of Pavonazzo marble from Pietrasanta, Italy. The choir stalls nearby were carved of English oak in Oberammergau, Germany, with each stall carved in a different design.

The altar is of the same material, with the top slab of Sienna marble. A small block of Jerusalem stone from the quarry of Solomon just north of the Damascus Gate is inserted in the center of the altar near the front. The reredos behind the altar is of carved stone and contains 59 statues of prominent figures in ancient and modern Christian history. The reredos was suggested in part by the one in Winchester Cathedral in England.

Trinity's windows are arranged to show the life of Christ, beginning with his birth and climaxing in his Resurrection. The series begins in the chapel and south transept. The large traceried window in this transept illustrates the Nativity, with Mary and Joseph adoring the Christ Child in the center panel. The windows in the south nave aisle depict scenes from the childhood of Jesus. The north aisle windows in the nave show notable events from the ministry of Jesus.

An unusual window is found in the north transept. It shows the scene of the Crucifixion in the upper panel and the entombment in the lower panel. An interesting feature is the use of medieval costumes for the figures. This use of costumes of a much later date than that of the time of Christ is characteristic of windows of the 1400s.[46] This window was created by an unknown Belgian artist and is a fine example of the use of silver in stained glass.

The window above the altar shows Christ enthroned surrounded by apostles, archangels and saints, including two early American bishops.

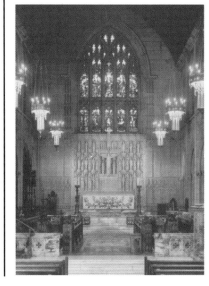

Cathedral Church of St. Paul, Peoria

Quincy
Mid America

St. Paul's Cathedral is one of the few in the Episcopal Church to be built in a contemporary style. It has won national awards both as an outstanding example of ecclesiastical architecture and for outstanding design in textile work.

When St. Paul's congregation moved into its new building in 1959, it marked a radical change from its previous home in a 19th century traditional edifice. Why a contemporary design? The word "contemporary" itself is part of the reason, since Christianity is a contemporary religion and, as such, should express itself in contemporary language. In addition, since funds were limited and space desired, a modern style was chosen.[47]

The brick, rectangular building with the altar in the center was designed by Frederick W. Dunn of the firm of Frederick Dunn and Associates in St. Louis. It was completed in March, 1959, dedicated October 4 of that year, and consecrated January 27, 1963. In 1968, an addition was placed at the east end of the building, providing space for offices, lounge and a hall.

When St. Paul's was built, it was a parish church. It continued in that status until 1967 when it was designated the cathedral by the Rt. Rev. Francis W. Lickfield. The previous cathedral was St. John's in Quincy, which had been organized as a parish in 1837 and became the cathedral in 1878.

A visitor to St. Paul's usually enters through the narthex. A large carpet is found there, hand-woven in Puerto Rico and suggesting the contours of the earth, the valleys and rivers created by God. The visitor then goes into the baptistry area. The baptismal font is a real clam shell, set on a base of Texas shell stone. A plexiglass canopy over the font contains symbols of the Holy Spirit. It was designed and made by Robert Harmon of the Emil Frei Studios of St. Louis.

The baptistry is under the organ gallery, which is supported by two columns. The columns were carved by William Donaldson, a local artist, and contain symbols of the apostles around the top, six on each column. The left column represents natural, physical creation and the right column is carved with symbols of the life hereafter.

The large window behind the loft contains many symbols of Christianity and is dominated by a large figure of St. Paul at the left. The window also was executed by Robert Harmon.

Another interesting carpet is found in the center aisle of the north nave, and is filled with representations of the fruits of the earth, especially those found in Illinois.

Flooring in the sanctuary and the altar pace are of slate. The altar is of Tennessee cedar marble with a figure of the phoenix, a symbol of the Resurrection, carved in the center on one side, and a pomegranate, a symbol of immortality, and a fish, an early symbol used to identify Christians, on the other side. The cross above the altar is of gold-leafed aluminum. On each side of the cross are five large pieces of red chunk glass, representing the five wounds in Christ's body.

Two pieces of marble which were removed from the credence tables in the old St. Paul's Church were used to construct the cathedral credence table.

The pulpit is of Etowah pink Georgia marble and has a sounding board of Philippine mahogany. The bishop's throne nearby is of pink marble. The wooden crucifix to the right was hand-carved in Oberammergau and installed in 1977.

On the wall of the south nave is a large Christ the King crucifix, which hung over the chancel in the old St. Paul's. It was carved and polychromed in Oberammergau and contains symbols of the four evangelists on the ends of the cross.

South Dakota
Mid America

A substantial gift from philanthropist John Jacob Astor was the seed which developed into Calvary Cathedral.

Calvary parish was begun in 1872, before statehood for South Dakota, when the Rev. W.H. Ross organized a congregation. A church building was erected before the end of that year. Ten years later, Calvary Parish bought property and moved to its new site.

In 1887, William H. Hare, first Bishop of South Dakota, was offered a substantial gift by Astor for the purpose of building "a church of permanent character, not so expensive as to be a burden for its support in a new country," as a memorial to his wife, the late Charlotte Augusta Astor.[48]

Astor asked Bishop Hare to secure land for the church and rectory which he would build, and specified that the church must be named the Church of St. Augusta. Astor also offered to furnish the chancel, pews, heating system, communion plate and organ.

Sioux Falls was chosen by Bishop Hare as the location for the new church. The cornerstone was laid December 5, 1888, and the building was dedicated December 18, 1889. A year later, Bishop Hare organized the Chapter of Calvary Cathedral, a holding corporation, to take title of all missionary property in the district. When the chapter was incorporated, Bishop Hare transferred title to the property on which St. Augusta's was located.

Members of Calvary Parish organized as a corporation in 1891. That brought about an unusual situation—Bishop Hare had a church building (St. Augusta's) without a congregation, and a parish (Calvary) without a church building. The bishop then invited parishioners of Calvary to worship in his cathedral and to occupy the rectory. The parish of Calvary Cathedral has occupied the Church of St. Augusta ever since.

A bronze table with the name Calvary Cathedral is displayed in the building more prominently than the cornerstone of St. Augusta's.

Inside, a visitor's attention is drawn to the altar and reredos which were installed in 1946. The reredos was given by parishioners as a thanksgiving for the life of Bishop W. Blair Roberts, and contains a beautifully carved figure of Christ the King in the central panel.

Some interesting crosses are found in the building. When Bishop Hare attended the 1888 Lambeth Conference, he was given two crosses, one of stone made from the walls of St. Augustine's Abbey, Canterbury, the remains of the oldest church in England. The other was a cross of polished jasper from the pavement of Canterbury Cathedral, brought to England from Italy by William the Conqueror in the 11th century. The crosses are found in the sanctuary floor and the altar slab.

Another noteworthy acquisition is the Jerusalem cross, mounted on a plaque above the credence table in the sanctuary. It is made from two small pieces of the rood from the Church of the Holy Sepulchre in Jerusalem.

The large window in the west end of the cathedral is in memory of Bishop Hare. The window shows how the Episcopal Church came to South Dakota.

Other improvements occurred in 1953, when a new educational building was completed; in 1961, when a carillon was installed; in 1978, when a new narthex was completed; and in 1979, with renovation and repair.

Work began in 1991 on a two-story addition to the cathedral which will provide additional classroom and fellowship space as well as offices for the Diocese of South Dakota.

Southern Ohio
Mid America

Without a cathedral for 65 years, the Diocese of Southern Ohio celebrated the 175th anniversary of Christ Church when it established the parish as its cathedral February 24, 1993. Christ Church succeeds St. Paul's Cathedral, demolished in 1928.

In 1817 Philander Chase, a missionary priest from Hartford, Connecticut, preached at a meeting in a Cincinnati Presbyterian church. He invited anyone interested in forming an Episcopal congregation to join him in a nearby home following that meeting. Twenty-one men attended and signed a document naming the congregation Christ Church. Among the signers was William Henry Harrison, ninth president of the United States. Christ Church at first rented space in a Baptist Church, later bought the building, then sold it to pay for the land on which the current cathedral is situated.

After eleven years the first rector, Samuel Johnston, resigned and organized another parish—St. Paul's—taking about half the congregation with him.

In 1836, a new Christ Church building was consecrated. It cost about $50,000 and served the congregation for more than a century.

In 1884 the Diocese of Southern Ohio was formed, held its convention at St. Paul's Church, and elected Thomas A. Jagger as its first bishop.

Isaac Newton Stanger, who was called to Christ Church as rector in 1877, criticized the parish and other churches in the vicinity for "failure to meet the needs for their services in the changing times." He urged the congregation to establish an endowment fund and to remain in the city's center. A trust fund to establish an endowment was formed in 1880, and that fund has grown to more than $30 million today.

During the latter part of the 19th century, the parish flourished, with many social ministries carried out and more than 500 families in the membership.

By 1906, the congregation had grown too large for its parish house. Mary Emery offered to build in memory of her husband, and a six-story building and tower were constructed and continue to be used.

The parish celebrated its centennial in 1917 and Mrs. Emery and the Charles Taft family contributed an English-style chapel, now located behind the church.

When Henry W. Hobson was consecrated fourth bishop in 1930 the service took place in Christ Church because the old cathedral had been torn down. For a time, Bishop Hobson used a "mobile cathedral," towing a converted mobile home behind his automobile to use as a chapel when visiting rural areas.

In 1937, Cincinnati was plagued by a massive flood of the Ohio River. Christ Church became a center for refugees, with the parish house becoming a dormitory, and hundreds of meals were served by volunteers.

Eighteen years later, the church needed considerable repairs. It was torn down to make room for a new edifice. The new brick church was dedicated on Palm Sunday, 1957.

In 1992 Herbert W. Thompson, eighth bishop, expressed his desire to establish Christ Church as a cathedral. "I hear God calling us to be more spiritually centered for the sake of the Episcopal Church, and for the sake of those in our midst," he said. "It is my hope that we can reach out to the city in the time of its needs and focus our concern for the city and diocese."[49]

Springfield
Mid America

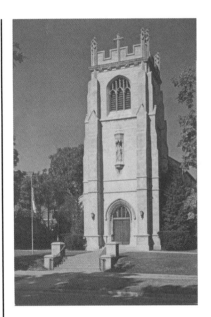

The diocese and the see city may be small, but St. Paul's Cathedral, Springfield, has a long and interesting history. St. Paul's was an early center of the Oxford Movement in this country, and has Abraham Lincoln listed in its marriage register.

Episcopal services were held in Springfield as early as 1832, but it wasn't until June 8, 1835 that a parish was organized. Bishop Philander Chase of the Diocese of Illinois met with a group which organized itself as St. Paul's parish. Bishop Chase left his nephew, Deacon Samuel Chase, in charge of the new congregation.[50]

For three years, the Episcopalians held services in local protestant churches. A small, frame church was ready for occupancy in August, 1838, and served the congregation until a new church was consecrated on June 25, 1848.

Rapid growth of the Episcopal Church in Illinois brought about the creation of new dioceses. The Diocese of Illinois was divided into Illinois (now Chicago), Quincy and Springfield, which consisted of 61 counties south of Chicago and east of the Illinois River.

St. Paul's began to reflect Anglo-Catholic practices during the latter part of the 19th century. The Holy Eucharist was celebrated daily, with a Choral Eucharist on Sundays. Candles appeared on the altar, confessions were introduced, and in all probability incense was used on feast days.[51]

Deterioration of the old church building led to discussions about a new church and location. Groundbreaking was held for a new church June 24, 1913, and the cornerstone was laid September 21 of that year. The first service in that building, which is now the cathedral, was held March 20, 1914, Maundy Thursday. John Sutcliffe of Chicago was architect for the building, which was designed in English perpendicular Gothic.

The possibility of a cathedral for the Diocese of Springfield was raised long before St. Paul's was elevated to that status. In 1877, when the Diocese of Springfield was established, Bishop George F. Seymour from time to time used the term "pro-cathedral" in designating St. Paul's as the principal church of the diocese. In 1891, he suggested to diocesan leaders that there should be a true "bishop's church," but no action was taken at that time.[52]

In 1943, Bishop John C. White noted in his address to diocesan synod that he had chosen St. Paul's as his official church, and from henceforth it would be known as the "pro-cathedral."[53]

For the next 25 years, various attempts were made to clarify the status of St. Paul's. On December 11, 1979, a constitution and by-laws were adopted, establishing the "Cathedral Church of St. Paul," administered by bishop, dean and chapter. Thus official action finally was taken, even though parish records show St. Paul's being recognized as the cathedral as early as 1906.[54]

Among the interior appointments is a handsome carved reredos behind the high altar. The reredos was carved by Alois Lang of Oberammergau.

Stained glass windows are done in medieval Gothic style using imported glass. All but one of the cathedral's 25 windows were designed by the Willet Studio of Philadelphia over the last 70 years.

The oldest window is the one above the high altar and reredos and depicts the beatific vision. The most recent windows are the three at the rear of the nave dedicated on Pentecost, 1982, by Bishop Donald Hultstrand.

A campaign of restoration, preservation and enhancement of the cathedral was begun in 1990.

Cathedral of Christ the King, Kalamazoo

Western Michigan
Mid America

Western Michigan's cathedral is a contemporary structure visible to millions who drive along Interstate Highway 94 in the southern part of the state.

St. Mark's Church, Grand Rapids, served as the cathedral from 1942, but the diocese voted at its 1965 convention to build a new cathedral. Kalamazoo had been designated as the see city of the diocese the previous year.

Three weeks after the convention took that action, land was purchased along Interstate 94, approximately 140 miles from Detroit and 140 miles from Chicago. The firm of Irving W. Colburn and Associates of Chicago was chosen to design the building, and ground was broken July 30, 1967.

Original plans called for a larger building. Eventually a decision was made to build a smaller building, but of the same contemporary design.[55]

A congregation was organized by Bishop Charles E. Bennison in the spring of 1967, and a cathedral corporation was established.

In 1968, Bishop Bennison spoke of his vision for the cathedral: "The strong dynamic center I envisioned and preached would have to be a church first and foremost, housing at its heart the altar, with the various related aspects of the total mission of the church going out as spokes from the altar hub to all parts of the world, represented by the diocese."

The cathedral was completed in 1969 at a cost of more than $1.6 million and was dedicated by Bishop Bennison October 26 of that year. It was paid for by 1977 and consecrated by Bishop Bennison.

In an article prepared for people touring the cathedral, the Rev. Canon Don M. Gury wrote: "This late 20th century building of brick and glass on structural steel is a powerful statement of our faith in God. It is a functional workshop and power plant where godly men and women may labor together to bring the reign of Christ into our society."

The motif of the building is the circle in the square, and is repeated many times throughout the cathedral. It represents God in our world.

A large monument outside represents man's world. Allegorically depicted in bas-reliefs are commerce, agriculture, industry and the arts, major forces in the development of the Midwest in the early 20th century. The monument contains bas-reliefs which were on the facade of a downtown Chicago office building from 1922-52.

The building has 16 towers outside which form a kingly crown. Each tower splits to form two turrets.

A large, round white altar is the focal point of the square interior. A round skylight in the square ceiling above the altar symbolizes the Incarnation, with the light of Christ coming down into humanity's dark world.

The circle in the square theme is repeated at the baptismal font, the shape of the chapels (St. Mary's and the Chapel of the Holy Spirit) and other small chambers in the towers.

An interesting pattern of seating includes the bishop's throne to the north of the altar with stalls for the dean and canons on both sides. Chairs for the congregation are arranged around the altar in concentric circles, a reminder of the ripples caused by a pebble dropped into a pool.

The roof is supported by four steel girders resting on four pillars, which are named for the four evangelists.

Offices of the bishop and his staff are found on the outer walls. Other offices and a library are on the balcony level, and a parish hall and other rooms are in the undercroft.

Wyoming
Mid America

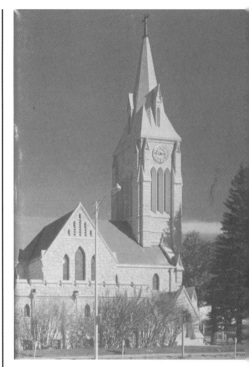

Wyoming's cathedral origins go back to a log cabin which served as the place of worship for the congregation during its early years.

St. Matthew's was the first church founded in Laramie, September 21, 1868, the Feast of St. Matthew. The Rev. Joseph Cook of Cheyenne visited Laramie that year and held a service in a dance hall. Cook's diary noted that the building of a church was delayed by a scarcity of lumber.[56]

Regular services began later in 1868 in a little log cabin which served as a public school during the day.[57]

A lot was given to St. Matthew's for its first church building, which was dedicated September 21, 1869, exactly one year after the congregation's founding. That first church was a small frame building on the site of the present cathedral. By 1881, St. Matthew's was self-supporting.

In 1887 Ethelbert Talbot became the first Bishop of the Missionary District of Wyoming and Idaho, and selected Laramie as his see city. Bishop Talbot felt a cathedral was needed and chose St. Matthew's. The little building was hardly of cathedral proportions, and it was decided to erect a new one.

Construction began in 1892 and continued until its first service was held December 23, 1896. The cathedral is of early English Gothic style, built of silicious limestone quarried near Laramie. Unlike most cathedrals, its axis is north-south.

Only 14 months after the new building opened, it was hit by fire. In February, 1898, the organ and woodwork caught fire, causing great damage. Enough contributions were received so that all the woodwork in the cathedral was replaced and the organ rebuilt. The church was consecrated in 1901.

When the Diocese of Wyoming became a separate jurisdiction in 1909, Nathaniel S. Thomas became its first bishop.

Bishop Thomas had a plan to build a great and dominant square in the city of Laramie "with homes for the bishop, archdeacon and dean, schools for boys and girls, a seminary and a library."[58]

Bishop Thomas was able to obtain several major gifts, and over the next 20 years he was able to establish a home for children, a school for boys, a school for girls, an Episcopal Club at the University of Wyoming, and a summer school for church workers. Much of what he had accomplished disappeared after he left in 1927.

St. Matthew's is dominated by a tower with spire and cross at the front of the building and two other flanking towers near the north end.

The nave is divided into five bays with a shallow transept on each side. The Chapel of Our Saviour parallels the west transept and northwest aisle and is separated by glass screens and doors. The roof of the nave and choir are open-timbered of a hammer beam style of construction.

Windows in the cathedral date from the opening of the building to 1962. One of the most striking is the Te Deum window above the high altar and reredos and the oak paneling of the sanctuary. A window portraying the cathedral's patron saint, Matthew, is found above the pulpit and shows Jesus calling Matthew from his tax collector's desk to be a disciple. It was designed by the Heaton, Butler and Bayne Studio.

Another interesting window is found to the south of the west arch and memorializes the ministry of the church in Wyoming. It was designed by Rowan and Irene LeCompte, installed in 1962 and includes ranchers, railroaders, students, Bishop Talbot and others.

Southeast

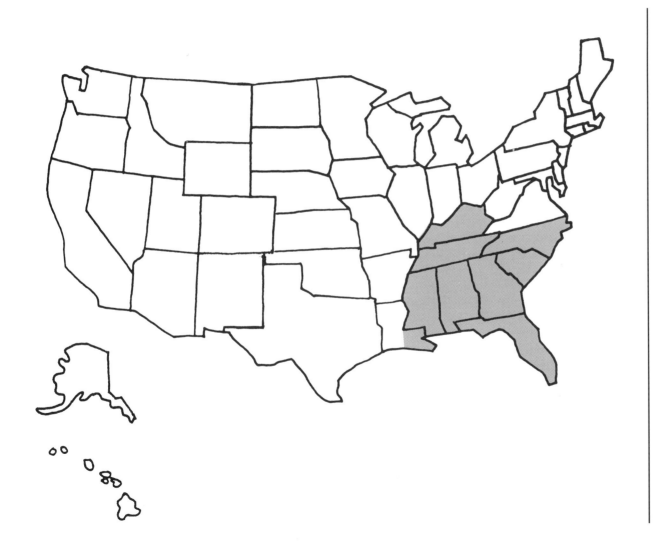

The Dioceses of

Atlanta
Alabama
Central Florida
East Tennessee
Florida
Kentucky
Lexington
Louisiana
Mississippi
South Carolina
Southeast Florida
Southwest Florida
Upper South Carolina
West Tennessee

Atlanta
Southeast

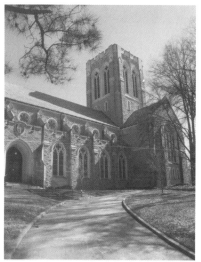

St.Philip's is home to the largest congregation in the Episcopal Church, with more than 5,000 communicants.[1]

The parish was established in 1847 with five communicants. A small wooden church was consecrated the following year by Stephen Elliott, first Bishop of Georgia.

During the Civil War the church was used for a variety of activities. In 1861 the congregation was organized into a "Hospital Aid Society," distributing supplies and using the church building as a hospital for wounded Confederate soldiers. After Gen. William T. Sherman's Union forces captured Atlanta, the building was used as a bowling alley for northern troops and as a barn for cavalry horses. The rectory, parish office building and two other small buildings were destroyed and the materials used to build federal barracks and fortifications. When Sherman's troops burned much of Atlanta, St. Philip's and four other nearby churches were spared.

On January 14, 1866, Bishop Elliott, using an Irish prayer book, performed the office for expiation and illustration of a church desecrated or profaned.

Another crisis occurred in 1878 when a tornado hit the church during a Sunday service. The walls and roof collapsed on the congregation, but, amazingly, no one was injured.[2]

That little wooden building was replaced in October, 1882, by a larger brick building of Gothic design, located on the same site. On May 6, 1897, that church was designated as the cathedral of the Diocese of Georgia. It was consecrated on the Feast of St. Philip and St. James, May 1, 1904. When the Diocese of Georgia split in two in 1907, St. Philip's became the cathedral for the new Diocese of Atlanta.

Because of financial problems and movement of members in the late 1920s, it was decided to sell the site of the old cathedral and erect a smaller building. A temporary wooden pro-cathedral was built in a residential area at an approximate cost of $10,000. It was dedicated September 10, 1933, as the pro-cathedral of the diocese by Bishop Henry J. Mikell.

The little gray building served the congregation until Thanksgiving Day, 1959, when the congregation began worshiping in what is now the Hall of Bishops. DeOvies Memorial Hall was built in 1951 to house the diocesan and cathedral offices.

The first service in the new cathedral was Easter Day, 1962. It was dedicated May 13, 1962, and consecrated March 16, 1980. Francis P. Smith is the architect. The building is constructed of Tennessee quartzite and trimmed with Indiana limestone.

The interior of St. Philip's is a traditional cruciform plan with nave, crossing, transepts and choir. The altar is of green and white Italian marble with a handsome reredos behind. The pulpit has a distinctive canopy and was built especially for the chancel. A Canterbury cross and a cross of nails hang on the walls to the right and left of the chancel steps, symbolizing the relationship between the cathedral and the worldwide Anglican Communion, with an emphasis on reconciliation.[3]

The baptistry, located in the narthex, contains a marble font which dates from 1882 and was brought from St. Philip's Church.

St. Philip's is blessed with some lovely stained glass windows. The windows in the cathedral and Mikell Chapel were designed by the Willet Studios of Philadelphia, those in the ambulatory and dean's study by Payne Stained Glass Associates of Paterson, New Jersey.

On the north wall in the balcony is the large "Benedicite"

rose window, a memorial to the 130 persons, most of them from Atlanta, who were killed in a plane crash in Paris in 1962. The 10 nave aisle windows illustrate various scenes from Christ's life. The 14 rose-shaped windows in the clerestory follow the development of Christianity by illustrating a significant person from each of the first 14 centuries.

Large windows dominate both transepts. In the east transept, acts of the Apostles and other personalities of the early church are shown. The west transept window traces the history of the Episcopal Church. The nine lancet windows in the chancel show more events from Christ's life.

Three chapels are found in St. Philip's. Mikell Memorial Chapel, near the narthex, was the first part of the cathedral to be completed, in 1947. It seats 100 and is used for daily services. St. Mary's Chapel is located in the undercroft, and contains furnishings from the old cathedral. And the Children's Chapel is in DeOvies Hall.

The cathedral organ is a four-manual, 98-rank Aeolian-Skinner, which was built in 1962 and overhauled in 1991.

Alabama

Southeast

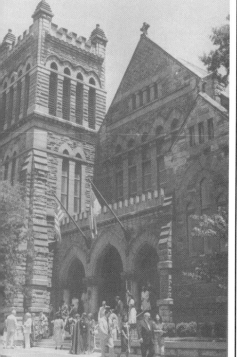

The Church of the Advent and the city of Birmingham were founded in the same year, 1872, more than 100 years before the parish became a cathedral.

The first two bishops of Alabama, Nicholas H. Cobbs and Richard H. Wilmer, had vision for the church in Birmingham. Bishop Cobbs had an idea for a cathedral as early as 1835. He foresaw a great church with carefully-planned and well-executed worship, a school for children, a program to care for the sick and to provide shelter for those in need. He even drew a sketch of a proposed cathedral and described its various ministries.[4] In 1877, his successor, Bishop Wilmer, envisioned for the Church of the Advent "a building which in its massiveness shall set forth her enduring principles, the strength of her towers and the beauty of her palaces."

The group which organized the congregation held services on Sunday afternoons as a mission church of St. John's, Elyton. Services were held on the second floor of a merchandise store which was used weekdays as an amusement hall.[5]

The lot on which the cathedral now sits was purchased in 1871 for $5. The president and chief engineer of the Elyton Land Company, which laid out the city, were members of the Church of the Advent, and devoted considerable time to its construction.

A small, frame Gothic church was built on the eastern corner of that lot in 1872 and was the first church building erected within the original city limits. A wing was added to it in 1886. The first church was destroyed by fire on Thanksgiving Day, November 24, 1892.

The foundation of the present building was laid in 1888, but work moved slowly, even stopping for a time because of lack of finances. The first service was held in 1893, three years before the structure was completed, and the church was consecrated April 9, 1899, by Henry M. Jackson, Bishop Coadjutor of Alabama. A parish house was added in 1908 and an addition was made to that building in 1923.

Even though it had not yet achieved cathedral status, the Church of the Advent functioned much like a cathedral. When Bishop William G. McDowell was consecrated in 1922, the service was held there and he maintained his headquarters there as well.[6]

Interior renovation of the church took place in 1936, and Meyer Chapel, which is used for weekday services, was added in 1951. In 1954, the diocese built Carpenter House to serve as diocesan headquarters.[7]

Following the consecration of Furman Stough as Bishop of Alabama in 1971, the church's centennial year, there was talk of establishing the Church of the Advent as the cathedral, but Bishop Stough said he'd talk about that plan later.[8]

In 1981, the Diocesan Convention, meeting at the Church of the Advent, authorized the Diocesan Council to negotiate an agreement with the parish to establish it as the cathedral. A year later, February 12, 1982, the parish was formally set apart at a service attended by Presiding Bishop John M. Allin.

The church, located among downtown high-rise office buildings, is an 18th century modified English Gothic cruciform style, constructed of non-porous Indiana sandstone.

Inside, wood predominates, especially the carved oak altar, delicately carved pulpit and handsome wainscoting.

In 1992, plans were made for a $4 million capital funds campaign to renovate all the buildings and to expand classroom and office space.

Central Florida
Southeast

St. Luke's has served as the cathedral for three jurisdictions of the Episcopal Church. First, for the Missionary District of South Florida, then the Diocese of South Florida, and, finally, for the Diocese of Central Florida.

Episcopal services were held regularly in Orlando for the first time in the early 1870s. Priests came to Orlando by horse and buggy from the nearby communities of Longwood and Sanford to conduct services in a free church/school building.

The site of the present cathedral was purchased in 1882 for $300, and a small, frame church building was erected. The mission church became St. Luke's parish April 28, 1884. In 1892, the church was consecrated by Edwin G. Weed, Bishop of Florida.

Later that year, the General Convention of the Episcopal Church created the Missionary District of South Florida, and William C. Gray was elected its first bishop. Bishop Gray decided to make Orlando his headquarters, and St. Luke's was designated the cathedral for the missionary district March 31, 1902.

St. Luke's experienced rapid growth and the building was expanded and parish programs increased. In 1922, the missionary district became a diocese, and the first diocesan convention was held at St. Luke's in 1923.

The old church was moved to another part of the same tract of land in October, 1922, in order that construction could begin on a new cathedral. The firm of Frohman, Robb and Little of Boston, which had designed Washington Cathedral, was hired as the architect.

Bishop Cameron Mann laid the cornerstone April 13, 1925. The first service was held April 3, 1926, Easter Eve, in a building which was only partially completed. The Depression had come early to Florida, and economic conditions made it impossible to complete construction, so a temporary wall sealed the east end.

The economic hardships began to ease during the 1930s, and an educational unit was constructed in 1945 as a memorial to members of the cathedral who died in World War II.

In 1970, the Diocese of South Florida was divided into three dioceses—Central, Southeast and Southwest Florida. St. Luke's continued as a cathedral, this time for the new Diocese of Central Florida.

The cathedral interior is dominated by the 15-foot hanging crucifix over the high altar. The crucifix was designed by Wippell Mowbray Ltd. of Exeter, England, and carved of limewood by DeMetz and Son Studio of Ortesi, Italy. The oak altar is designed by the same English firm and was dedicated at the same time as the crucifix, October 19, 1980.

The pulpit was installed in 1926 and was built by Angelo Lualdi, Inc., of Cambridge, Massachusetts, with the figures of outstanding preachers carved by Ernest Pellegrini. The carved oak lectern is one of the oldest appointments in the cathedral.

One of the most beautiful windows in St. Luke's is the one in the sanctuary depicting Christ enthroned in glory. It was installed in 1947, designed by the Willet Studio of Philadelphia, and enlarged in 1987 to a diameter of 12 1/2 feet. The rose window above the choir gallery was designed by Henry L. Willet and portrays the Benedicite canticle. It was dedicated in 1956.

St. Mary's Chapel contains some interesting furnishings. The altar and reredos served as the original high altar in the early Cathedral of St. Luke after having been used as the high altar at St. Clement's, Philadelphia, for 25 years. The three-lancet stained glass window above the reredos is dedicated to the Virgin Mary and the theme of family.

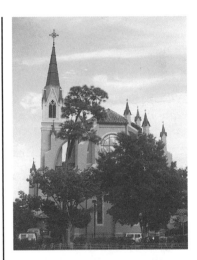

East Tennessee
Southeast

St. John's is one of the newest cathedrals of the Episcopal Church, having been designated in 1986 following a 142-year history as a parish.

In 1844, St. John's was organized as the sixth parish of the Diocese of Tennessee and the first in the city of Knoxville. The following year, a small, brick church was constructed on the same site as the present cathedral. That building was enlarged in 1879, and the parish reported considerable activity, with an orphanage already begun, along with another mission church.

By 1890, the original church was too small for the congregation, and construction began the next year on a new edifice. The last service in the old church was held in June, 1891, before it was razed. The new building was dedicated in 1892. The structure was made of Georgia marble, with every stone cut and numbered at the quarry, then taken to Knoxville for ease of assembly.

The present altar, pulpit and chancel rail were given as memorials when the new church, which is now the cathedral, was opened. Other appointments were brought from the original building. The window above the Walnut Street door had been above the altar in the first church, and the lectern and font also were moved from the earlier St. John's.

During the years of World War I, the parish house and chapel were constructed.

In 1919, a fire caused by ignition of soft coal used in the furnace caused extensive damage to St. John's, especially to many memorial windows.

Further growth occurred during the 1950s. A wing on the parish house was constructed in 1950, and the Church of the Ascension was dedicated in 1957. Ascension was intended to be a chapel of St. John's, but it soon achieved parish status.

A major renovation took place in 1963-64. The basement was excavated under the church, and the interior contents, including the floor, were removed. The congregation was out of the building for a year. During that time, some services were held where the library now stands, others at Tyson House, part of the complex.

Additional work was done in 1980, when the parish house wing was renovated to provide offices and classrooms, and improvements were made to the chapel. A parish hall was constructed of the same marble and stone pattern as the church, and connected to the church and parish house.

In 1985, the Diocese of East Tennessee was created out of the Diocese of Tennessee, with William E. Sanders as its first bishop. St. John's became the cathedral for the new diocese December 4, 1986.

A recent addition to the complex was the construction of the Diocesan Center in 1988.

Looking toward the altar, one is sure to notice a mosaic of the Ascension of Christ set into the rear wall above the altar. At the other end of the church is a window depicting the Apostles watching the Ascension. The large rose window was hand-crafted by Wippell Company of London and installed in 1989. It represents the seven sacraments and replaced the plain glass upper portion of windows damaged in the 1919 fire.

Three groups of windows are found in the north transept. The windows are representative of the Trinity and were brought from the original St. John's.

The mural decorations of the vaulted chancel ceiling and the murals in the nave were executed by Hugh Tyler, who grew up as a member of St. John's before moving to New York City. The original paintings were destroyed by the fire, and Tyler made new designs.

Florida
Southeast

The complex of St. John's Cathedral and its accompanying buildings fill four square blocks in downtown Jacksonville.

St. John's was incorporated in April, 1834, in a general act approved by the Legislature of the Territory of Florida. The cornerstone of the first building was laid April 24, 1842, and marked the first of three church buildings to occupy that site.

The first St. John's was consecrated April 18, 1851, by Stephen Elliott, Bishop of Georgia.

The church building wound up being used as a hospital for Union soldiers. On Sunday, March 29, 1863, soldiers burned St. John's to the ground, then boarded boats in the St. Johns River and sailed away. Parish records note that Dr. Alfred Walton, a federal medical officer, ran into the burning church and "took from the altar a large gilt-bound prayer book with the inscription on the cover 'St. John's Episcopal Church in Jacksonville.'" Three years later, Dr. Walton returned the book to the parish.

The cornerstone for the second church building was laid April 7, 1874. The first service was held on Easter Day, April 1, 1877. The church was consecrated May 7, 1882, by Bishop John F. Young of Florida.

Tragedy struck again May 3, 1901, when all of the buildings were destroyed by fire. A small, wooden chapel was erected on the site following the fire, which destroyed much of Jacksonville.

The congregation began to rebuild quickly, and the cornerstone for what is the present cathedral was laid February 18, 1903. It was dedicated by Bishop Edwin G. Weed on Easter Day, 1906, and consecrated in 1911.

The new building, designed by Snelling and Potter of New York City, was of Gothic style typical of English parish churches. The exterior is of Indiana limestone and the roof of Pennsylvania slate.

Other buildings in the complex were erected in 1929, 1964 and 1971 and in harmony with the cathedral in style and ornamentation.

St. John's became the cathedral for the Diocese of Florida in 1951, under Bishop Frank A. Juhan.

The interior of the cathedral was completely renovated in 1983 in anticipation of the 150th anniversary of incorporation as a parish. That celebration was held on Palm Sunday, 1984. The architect, W. Stanley Gordon, said the changes produced "one of the finest liturgical settings in this country for a eucharistically-centered church."[9]

The new carved oak woodwork was created by W. Herbert Reid, Ltd. of Exeter, England. The bishop's throne is a wooden replica of St. Augustine's chair in Canterbury Cathedral. The pews replaced original high back pews, but their appearance is identical to the former pews, and the old pew numbers were placed on the new pew ends.

Many of the stained glass windows were made by the Payne Studios of New Jersey. Windows of note: at the west end is a Tiffany window which portrays Christ the Good Shepherd and is the oldest window in the cathedral; the seven-panel nave windows showing the life of Christ; the rose window over the west doors, which was made in Munich, Germany, and installed in 1913; and the All Saints' window in the Chapel of the Holy Communion, installed in 1929, which contains a piece of blue glass from a shattered window of the bombed cathedral in Rheims, France.[10] The large rose window at the east end depicts Christ the Good Shepherd and was installed in 1925.

St. John's has produced nine bishops and four deans of other cathedrals.[11]

*Christ Church Cathedral,
Louisville*

Kentucky
Southeast

Christ Church Cathedral's congregation has worshiped on the same site, in essentially the same building, for more than 165 years.

Episcopal services were held in Louisville as early as 1803, when a small group gathered with the Rev. Williams Kavanagh in a rough-hewn log building. A church was organized May 31, 1822, when nine men gathered in a local hall. Two months later, a second meeting was held with the name Christ Church chosen.

The first church building was erected in 1824, a two-story brick structure, nearly square in shape, based on the style of early federal meeting houses. A gallery was erected and a steeple and bell added in 1832. A major renovation took place in 1845, when the church was enlarged on the east end, providing a new chancel area.

When James Craik became rector in 1844, it marked the beginning of 74 years of leadership by the Craik family. James Craik was succeeded by his son, Charles E. Craik, in 1882.

In 1859, a second renovation enlarged the church further, and it was re-consecrated March 16, 1860. A new church was considered by the vestry in 1869, but it was decided instead to raise funds for the expansion and improvement of the existing building. In 1870, a west front of Kentucky limestone was added along with a narthex and two asymmetrical towers which flank a central gable, and replaced the original central tower. A fourth renovation took place in 1887, when the interior was redecorated.

Christ Church's becoming the cathedral for the Diocese of Kentucky was discussed as early as 1867, but cathedral status wasn't achieved until May 6, 1894.

As the renovations took place through the 19th century, the east end of the church was extended three times. The lines marking the end of the brick walls of the original church may be seen from the garden of the adjoining Cathedral House. Of the original 1824 building, the side walls of the nave and the timber-roof trusses remain.

Further improvements were made in 1919-22, when the chancel arch was moved, requiring additional columns, and remodeling and enlarging provided additional office space. Another renovation from 1951-56 included refurbishing of the exterior and redecorating of the interior.

Many of the memorials in the cathedral were added during the latter part of the 19th century. The altar and its reredos are of white Vermont marble with colored Italian marble. The altar originally was ordered by a Roman Catholic parish, but it was rejected on delivery in 1893 because the ornamental panels on each side of the figures of the Virgin Mary and St. John were reversed.[12]

There are 17 stained glass windows from the 19th century, including five from the Tiffany Studios, two from Heaton, Butler and Payne of London, and two of Munich design. The Tiffany windows are the last two on both aisles and the one by the organ.

The chapel is a recent addition to the cathedral and includes an interesting marble panel behind the altar and a large window designed by Kenneth Van Roenn Jr. of Louisville.

Christ Church Cathedral has been the host for a General Convention of the Episcopal Church, in 1973, and Anglicans from all over the world came to the cathedral in 1987 for the Partners in Mission Consultation of the Episcopal Church.

The cathedral achieved a first in 1987 when Geralyn Wolf was named dean, becoming the first woman in the Anglican Communion to be dean of a cathedral.

Lexington
Southeast

Christ Church, one of the Episcopal Church's newest cathedrals, has been a cathedral before, but returned to parish status for 56 years before its designation in 1989.

Christ Church is the oldest Episcopal Church in Kentucky, having been founded in 1796. The present building is the fourth on the site. It was erected in 1848 and enlarged to its present proportions during the Civil War.

During 1790-91, a group designated as "The Episcopal Society" had been meeting for worship in a log cabin four miles from the town of Lexington. This group was the nucleus of the first organized church.[13]

In 1796, the Rev. James Moore began to hold services in a "dilapidated little frame house" on the site of the present cathedral.[14]

A small, brick church was erected in 1803 to replace the frame house, and the parish was organized July 2, 1809.

Another new church was built in 1814. This was a larger brick building, stuccoed to resemble stone. The parish was named Christ Church in 1827, and the edifice was consecrated by Thomas C. Brownell, Bishop of Connecticut in 1829.

The Diocese of Kentucky was organized in 1829, and Benjamin B. Smith, rector of Christ Church, was elected as the first Bishop of Kentucky.

Four years later, a cholera epidemic swept through Lexington, and about a fourth of the parishioners died.[15]

The cornerstone of the present cathedral was laid on March 17, 1847, and the building was completed in 14 months. The edifice was plain Gothic in style, constructed of brick and colored with a wash of water, lime and sand. The nave was enlarged and transepts added in 1862-63.

A new diocese was created in 1895, when the Diocese of Lexington was formed out of the Diocese of Kentucky. Lewis

W. Burton became the first Bishop of Lexington in 1896, and the following year the Christ Church vestry and congregation offered the building as the cathedral. Bishop Burton accepted that offer and Christ Church became the cathedral in 1897.[16]

In 1933, Bishop H.P. Abbott decided to discontinue the designation of Christ Church as the cathedral, and it returned to parish status.

Shortly after Bishop William R. Moody was consecrated in 1945, he adopted an innovative plan for a Cathedral Domain in Eastern Kentucky, which later would become the site of the Cathedral of St. George the Martyr, a true cathedral in the center of the diocese.[17]

St. George's is a large wooden building in a rural setting and was constructed by four persons.[18] It continues to serve the diocese on a 700-acre site, with camps and conferences continuing to be held at the domain.

Christ Church returned to cathedral status August 1, 1989. In a service of establishment November 26, 1989, Bishop Don A.Wimberly said Christ Church "acted as a cathedral in every way, but now it's official."[19]

Some of the building's original furnishings remain in use. A marble baptismal font dates to 1848 when the church was opened. The 10 grisaille windows on the sides, each divided into three lancets, also are from 1848. The hexagonal-shaped pulpit and the lectern were installed in 1868.

Another window of note is the west window, which was designed by the Willet Studio of Philadelphia and installed in 1962. It depicts the verses of the Benedicite.

—Cathedral of St. George the Martyr

Christ Church Cathedral, New Orleans

Louisiana
Southeast

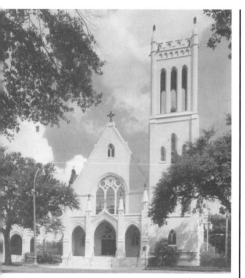

The Louisiana cathedral's founding parish, Christ Church, was the first non-Roman Catholic congregation in the Louisiana Purchase territory.

In June, 1805, 53 "protestants" met in New Orleans to form a religious association. When the group made plans to incorporate itself, those persons voted for a denomination of preference. The totals were: Episcopalian 45 votes, Presbyterian 7 and Methodist 1. The group then decided to name the congregation Christ's Church.[20]

Services were held in various public buildings until 1816 when the first church was built. The edifice was octagonal with a domed roof and a cupola. By 1835, the first building was too small for the growing congregation, so a second church was constructed on the same site, this one in the design of a Greek temple with columns. It was consecrated March 26, 1837.

A third building was constructed 12 years later. A Jewish congregation bought the second church and it became a synagogue.[21] The new church was Gothic in style with buttresses and a central tower. It served the congregation for 40 years.

During the latter part of the 19th century, most of Christ Church's parishioners lived in uptown New Orleans, so it was decided to build a new church in that area. The cornerstone for the present cathedral was laid June 10, 1886. Architect Lawrence B. Volk of New York City designed a stone Gothic building, cruciform in shape. Its first service was on Easter Day, 1887. A chapel was added in 1889.

Christ Church became a cathedral in 1891, when it was so designated by Davis Sessums, who became Bishop of Louisiana after having been rector of Christ Church.

A major expansion in 1959 provided space for offices, church school classes and an assembly hall. The addition was of the same Gothic style as the church.

The cathedral contains a variety of styles of stained glass windows, with nearly 100 windows in the church and chapel. One window was destroyed by a hurricane in 1965, and others were damaged and repaired. Among the interesting windows is the one over the main door, illustrating the nativity. It was made by the Burnham Studio of Boston and installed in 1953. The oldest windows are the three lancets over the door between the church and chapel which were brought from the third Christ Church.

The four windows above the choir represent the archangels and were installed in 1951 by the Howard Studios. The clerestory windows depict great Christians from St. Joseph of Arimathea to Bishop Samuel Seabury. Most of the windows were executed by the Willet Studios of Philadelphia and were installed between 1957 and 1981.

The cathedral's high altar contains stone fragments from Glastonbury Abbey, the English ruins where a great pilgrimage is held each June. It was installed in 1938. The bishop's throne was made between 1841 and 1867 by slaves on the plantation of Leonidas Polk, first Bishop of Louisiana, who was also a general in the Confederate army.

Harris Memorial Chapel has an altar stone given by the dean and chapter of Canterbury Cathedral. It contains fragments of Purbeck marble (A.D. 1200-1250).

The cathedral contains a bell cast in 1858 and originally installed in the third Christ Church. For many years it was electrically connected to the local fire station and alerted men of the area who were members of the volunteer fire department.[22]

Mississippi
Southeast

The congregation of Mississippi's cathedral has survived fires, a yellow fever epidemic, the Civil War and racial tensions, and emerged to celebrate its sesquicentennial in 1989.

St. Andrew's was founded in 1839 when David S. Lewis, a deacon, was sent to Jackson by the Domestic Missionary Society of the Episcopal Church.

The congregation was admitted to parish status in 1843 and held services in a Methodist church building. In 1845, a lot was purchased, and construction began on a building. On February 24, 1850, the feast of St. Matthias, the new building was consecrated by William M. Green, first Bishop of Mississippi.

St. Andrew's College was opened in 1852. When it closed four years later, Bishop Green directed the energies of himself and the Diocese of Mississippi toward the founding of the University of the South.[23]

The Civil War proved to be a tumultuous time for St. Andrew's. Mississippi withdrew from the Union in 1861, and the war came to Jackson in 1863, causing great devastation to the city. Bishop Green and the rector of St. Andrew's, William Crane, ministered to soldiers and civilians during the war.[24] A siege by Union troops occurred July 10-17. St. Andrew's was destroyed by fire, and many parish records were lost.

The congregation met in various places following the war, and the cornerstone for a new church was laid June 1, 1869, by Bishop Green. The new building was completed early in 1873.

The latter part of the 19th century brought growth and stability to St. Andrew's, and in 1901 plans were made for construction of a new church. P.H. Weathers, who grew up in Jackson, was selected as the architect. The new building,

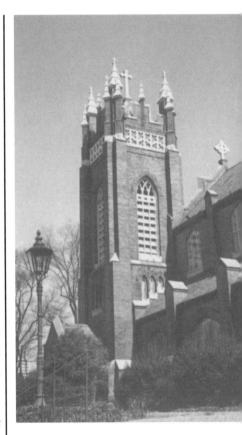

which is the present cathedral, was in use in the spring of 1903.

Another fire occurred on January 5, 1930, when the church roof was destroyed. The interior of the church was damaged by water. Repairs and renovation began immediately and a new Wurlitzer organ was installed. When the congregation gathered on Easter Day in 1930, the church was fully renovated and the new organ was in use.

In 1963, the racial tensions which existed in much of the South were experienced in Jackson. In June of that year, "kneel-ins" occurred on several Sundays. A racially-mixed group presented itself at the entrance of St. Andrew's and was admitted by the wardens and ushers without incident in accord with the tradition and practice that had existed at St. Andrew's from the beginning.[25] Parish records indicate blacks had worshiped at St. Andrew's as early as the 1850s.

On November 17, 1965, St. Andrew's accepted an invitation from Bishop Duncan Gray to become the cathedral, and a service of establishment was held January 19, 1966.

The dean of St. Andrew's, Robert G. Oliver, reported in 1974, "that during the previous year, St. Andrew's probably had the largest actual growth and percentage growth of any Episcopal cathedral in the United States."[26] At that time there were 1,600 baptized members and 1,275 communicants.

There are attractive examples of stained glass in St. Andrew's, many from the Willet Studio of Philadelphia. The apse clerestory windows, known as the "Bishops' Windows," depict the calling of the Apostles, the Last Supper and the great commission.

South Carolina
Southeast

South Carolina's cathedral sustained more than $2 million damage from Hurricane Hugo, which roared through the city in September, 1989. Worship services were held in the parish house for more than a year.

The cathedral can trace its beginning to 1806, when a mission was organized as the Third Episcopal Church of Charleston. That congregation held its services in the French Church from 1810-1815. Two years later, at the 29th convention of the Diocese of South Carolina, the Third Church was referred to for the first time as St. Paul's.[27]

The cornerstone for the present cathedral was laid November 9, 1811, and the building was consecrated March 28, 1816 by Theodore Dehore, second Bishop of South Carolina, making it the second oldest building among Episcopal cathedrals still in use. The edifice, designed by James and John Gordon, was traditional for that period and includes a portico with four Doric columns supporting an angular pediment and a modified Gothic tower. The tower was not part of the Gordons' plan, which called for a steeple. The foundation for the steeple proved to be inadequate, and cracks began to appear in the structure; the tower was substituted. The tower once had a bell, but it was surrendered to the Confederate government during the Civil War to be use for cannons.[28]

Extensive renovation took place both inside and outside in 1838, and another remodeling was done shortly before the Civil War. The church was closed for a time during that war. In 1872, the high boxed pews were replaced, the crossing eliminated and the pulpit moved from the center of the chancel to the north side.

Meanwhile, St. Luke's parish was going through its early years. That parish was founded in 1857, and a temporary chapel was built the following year. In 1859, the cornerstone was laid for a church building, and that was consecrated February 15, 1862. The church was struck by a shell from a federal battery October 7, 1864, and sustained major damage. It was stripped by troops, then used for political meetings, then as a school for black students.[29]

In 1904, Louis Wood left St. Paul's to become rector of St. Luke's and many of St. Paul's members followed. Attempts were made to merge the two congregations, but that didn't take place until 1949. At that time, the vestry of St. Paul's invited the vestry of St. Luke's to explore possibilities of a merger. They agreed, with St. Paul's selected as the building and the rector of St. Luke's as the new rector.[30] The first service of the combined congregation was held July 17, 1949.

Negotiations were held in 1961-63 to establish the parish of St. Luke and St. Paul as the cathedral, and agreement finally was reached September 20, 1963.

A redecoration of the chancel took place in 1975. Windows in the chancel were covered by plywood panels, and a large tau cross now dominates the center panel, flanked by bas relief figures of St. Luke and St. Paul, designed and executed by Emmett Robinson.

One of the architectural features of the cathedral is the great arch leading to the apse and dominated by the large wooden cross. The bishop's chair is centered behind the altar. The nave has two rows of lofty, arched windows on each side.

The cathedral was re-consecrated February 21, 1991, during diocesan convention following the renovation required after the hurricane.[31]

Southeast Florida
Southeast

Trinity Cathedral has come a long way from its early days in a building known affectionately by members as "Church of the Holy Cheesecloth" to today's splendid building.

Trinity was begun in 1893 when Bishop William C. Gray of the Missionary Jurisdiction of Florida was invited to celebrate the Eucharist in the parlor of the home of Julia D. Tuttle, one of Miami's "pioneers." The church was incorporated in 1896, and Mrs. Tuttle donated land for a church building. A simple frame structure was built, complete with cheesecloth screens to keep out mosquitos and sand flies.

The congregation was established as a parish by the Rev. Nathaniel B. Fuller, who was sent to Miami by Bishop Gray in 1899. The little frame church was soon outgrown, and a second church was constructed in 1911 on the same site, a Victorian-style, gabled concrete building.

When a building boom hit South Florida in the early 1920s, Trinity expanded rapidly as northerners moved to Miami, and in 1923 the vestry decided to build another church. Architect Harold H. Mundy was contracted, and designed an unusual Romanesque revival structure, which was completed in 1925 in the residential suburb of Miramar.

A year later, Miami was struck by a killer hurricane, the boom went bust, and the Depression, which hit Florida before the rest of the nation, set in. Suddenly, the future of the congregation and its new building were in doubt. There were few tourists, a dwindling congregation and a large debt to face. The parish went into receivership, and gave its bayfront property behind the church to the bank, which reduced the mortgage, forgave unpaid interest and reduced the interest rate.[32]

Twenty years later, the debt was satisfied, and Trinity was consecrated June 16, 1946. Slow, steady growth and progress followed, and the parish was able to erect a new education building in 1957.

In 1970, the Diocese of South Florida was divided into three dioceses. The Miami area became part of the Diocese of Southeast Florida. Bishop James Duncan established Trinity as the cathedral for the new diocese on Easter Day, 1970.

Construction of the cathedral became complete in 1986, with the addition of the campanile called for in the original 1925 plans, but never constructed because of a lack of funds.

Architect Mundy's plan of Romanesque revival can be seen best in the wide nave, the rounded arches and the large window openings. The building's stained glass windows have a French Gothic look, and the mosaic encrustments remind a viewer of Byzantine architecture.

Mosaics are a feature of Trinity's interior. The 14 arches are bridged by spandrel mosaics which illustrate the way of the cross. Particularly striking is the apse, with a mosaic sunburst of light with angels and archangels on both sides depicting "the heavens and all the powers therein" from the canticle Te Deum. The mosaic encrustments on the triumphal arch over the altar portray the six days of creation in the oblong panels and the biblical symbols of the gospel writers in the circles.

The windows on the south side of the church tell the story of Christ's life, beginning at the east end with the Annunciation, and concluding at the west end with the Ascension. North side windows commemorate saints, monarchs and scholars of the Church in England, Ireland, Scotland and Wales.

Southwest Florida
Southeast

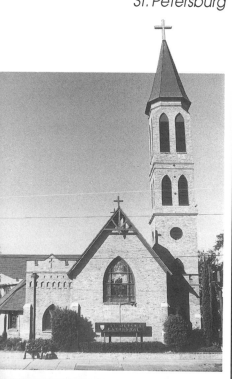

Southwest Florida's cathedral serves one of the fastest-growing dioceses in the Episcopal Church. In 1989, it marked 100 years of existence and 20 years as a cathedral.

St. Peter's was founded as an unorganized mission in 1889 when a few members of St. Bartholomew's Church began meeting. The mission became known as the Church of the Holy Spirit and soon had a small, wooden church of its own.

The mission was formally organized in March, 1894, by William C. Gray, Bishop of South Florida, and the church was named St. Peter's. The small building was moved to a new site and was used by the congregation for the next five years.

The present cathedral building was erected in 1899, and the original chapel was used as a parish house. St. Peter's achieved parish status in 1906, and a new parish house was built that year.

Considerable growth was recorded during the next 20 years, and in 1925-26, the parish renovated its building. The church was enlarged to double its size by extending the nave to the west, and by an extension to the south, forming a transept. That space later became St. Mary's Chapel.

St. Peter's observed its 25th anniversary in 1931, but then, like most churches at the time, went into financial doldrums in the Depression.[33] There was enough recovery for a new parish house to be built as the decade came to a close. That building was completed in 1940 along with cloisters which connect with the church and St. Mary's Chapel. A third floor was added to the parish house in 1958.

During 1953-59, growth in the Tampa Bay area was so rapid that six new Episcopal churches were formed in the St. Petersburg area. St. Peter's was affected by that growth as about 800 communicants left in order to help in the formation of the new parishes.[34]

The 80th year of St. Peter's existence, 1969, turned out to be of great significance to the parish. A major renovation of the interior of the church took place, and the Diocese of South Florida was divided into three dioceses. St. Petersburg was chosen as the see city for the new Diocese of Southwest Florida and St. Peter's Church was designated as the cathedral.

The centennial year was observed in 1989 with many events. Among the accomplishments was the refurbishing of the Austin organ, which had been installed in 1965.

The Florida Gothic design building contains some fine examples of stained glass. One of the most impressive is located at the east end above where the high altar originally stood. The window shows Christ walking on the water and is dated Easter, 1914. It has a wide border of leaves and scrolls in the style used in the medieval cathedrals of Europe.[35] The nine clerestory windows on the left side of the building depict the stations of the cross. The four on the other side portray the seven sacraments. The large window above the entrance represents The Lord Is My Shepherd from Psalm 23. Two large windows on the south side of St. Mary's Chapel illustrate the Te Deum and the Benedicite.

Windows installed since 1957 were fashioned by the Willet Studios of Philadelphia, the Payne Studios of Paterson, New Jersey, and the Wippell Glass Company of England.

Upper South Carolina

Southeast

Trinity Cathedral, Columbia

It has been a cathedral for only a short time, but Trinity has a long history, existing on the same corner in downtown Columbia since 1814.

Trinity Church was founded in 1812, when a group of Columbia residents incorporated themselves as a parish. Funds were raised with the help of the Protestant Episcopal Society to construct a small, wooden building which was dedicated in 1814.

In 1845, during the 52-year rectorate of Peter Shand, it was decided to build a new church. Edward B. White of Charleston was hired as the architect, and he designed a Gothic style building modeled after York Minster in England, with twin towers and pointed arches. It was consecrated in 1847. Transepts were built and the chancel was extended in 1861-62, during the early part of the Civil War.

The Union army, under General William T. Sherman, invaded Columbia February 17, 1865. A third of the city was in ashes by the following morning. Fires raged all around Trinity, but, miraculously, the church building was spared. The rectory and parish house, however, were destroyed by fire. Union soldiers came through the churchyard, and the communion silver was taken, never to be returned.[36]

On October 10, 1922, the Diocese of Upper South Carolina was formed, with Trinity becoming part of it.

Trinity functioned much like a cathedral for Upper South Carolina before achieving cathedral status. From 1922-1973, five bishops of Upper South Carolina were consecrated at Trinity.[37]

On January 19, 1977, Trinity was designated the cathedral by Bishop George M. Alexander.

Among the interesting appointments in the cathedral are the baptismal font, designed by sculptor Hiram Powers, the altar, made of Carrara marble, the box pews, which resemble those in the original Trinity, and the marble tablets in the sanctuary inscribed with the Lord's Prayer, Apostles' Creed and the Ten Commandments.

There are rose windows in both transepts. In the south transept, the seal of the Diocese of Upper South Carolina is at the center, and the petals describe the thoughts of Psalm 121. The north transept window portrays the sayings of Jesus, each beginning with "I am," with Jesus the Lamb of God at the center. The transept windows were created by the Willet Studios of Philadelphia.

The window over the altar illustrates Jesus gathering little children. The oldest windows in the nave are in the partition which separates the narthex from the main body of the church. The three windows on the right side of the aisle depict the Resurrection. The three on the left side are alpha and omega on both sides of a center lancet which glorifies music in worship.

The five windows on the left side of the church portray the life of Christ, and those on the right are scenes from the Acts of the Apostles. The Great West Window represents the Holy Trinity, and the clerestory windows all show scenes from the New Testament.

Trinity's property, which encompasses a square block, includes a historic cemetery which has graves of six governors, Revolutionary and Civil War heroes, seven bishops, distinguished scholars and civic leaders, and a Heisman Trophy-winning football star. The cemetery has a variety of trees and plants, including two cedar trees reportedly brought from Lebanon.

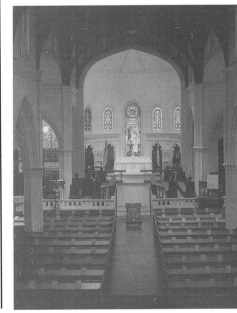

*St. Mary's Cathedral,
Memphis*

West Tennessee
Southeast

*St. Mary's Cathedral,
Memphis*

St. Mary's Cathedral has significance throughout the Episcopal Church. It was at St. Mary's where the little band of people serving the victims of yellow fever became the Martyrs of Memphis. The church's General Convention of 1985 added the Martyrs of Memphis to the Calendar of Lesser Feasts and Fasts. It is now observed September 9 each year.

St. Mary's was founded in 1857 as a mission of Calvary Church, Memphis, under the direction of James H. Ottey, first Bishop of Tennessee. A small, wooden, Gothic structure was erected, and dedicated in 1858. The house and lot next door were given as a residence for the bishop.

The proposal for St. Mary's to be the cathedral was discussed as early as 1860. It was made the cathedral January 1, 1871, by Bishop Charles Quintard.

In 1873, the Sisters of the Community of St. Mary were called to the cathedral by Bishop Quintard to operate the nearby Church Home for Orphans and to establish a school for girls at the cathedral.

During the summer of 1878, Memphis was struck by the third and most devastating yellow fever epidemic in a decade. More than 5,000 residents of Memphis (about a tenth of the city's population) died during the epidemic. St. Mary's was a center of service during the crisis.

On September 6 of that year, the Rev. Charles C. Parsons became the first of those associated with the cathedral to die from the epidemic. Two days later, Louis Schuyler, a volunteer priest from Hoboken, New Jersey, died. Sister Constance died September 9, Sister Theclan September 12, Sister Ruth September 18 and Sister Frances on October 4. Sister Hughetta Snowden survived until 1926.

The old wooden structure, which had served St. Mary's for 27 years, was torn down in 1898, and the cornerstone was laid for the present cathedral building. Bishop Thomas F. Gailor was the driving force behind the new building, having visited European cathedrals to secure ideas for St. Mary's.

The original architect for the new edifice was W. Halsey Wood of New York, one of the architects for New York's Cathedral of St. John the Divine. Architects who succeeded him were L. M. Weathers in 1905, and Bayard Snowden Cairns in 1925. A second cornerstone was laid in 1926 when the building was completed. The two cornerstones can be found at the sides of the front door. The cathedral is of modified 13th century English Gothic. The exterior is faced with white stone quarried on the mountain of Sewanee.

The oldest part of the cathedral complex is the Sisters Chapel, built in 1887 for the sisters, and St. Mary's School for Girls. It was renovated and refurnished in 1940.

St. Mary's contains some fine stained glass windows, all of which were designed by Len Howard of Kent, Connecticut. The tall lancet windows above the front door depict the Blessed Virgin Mary and St. John the Divine. The clerestory windows above the columns in the nave contain shields of all parishes in the Diocese of Tennessee in 1956. The windows above the sanctuary show the ascendant Christ surrounded by his apostles.

The high altar is made of Caen stone from a quarry in France, and Lisbon and Tennessee marble. It was installed in the old cathedral in 1879, and moved to the partially completed new building in 1905. The names of the four Sisters of St. Mary who died in the epidemic, and Sister Hughetta are engraved in the steps of the altar.

St. Mary's became the cathedral of the Diocese of West Tennessee in 1983, when the Diocese of Tennessee was divided into three dioceses.

Dioceses Without Cathedrals
(as of July 1993)

Alaska
Central Gulf Coast
East Carolina
Eastern Oregon
Fort Worth
Georgia
Los Angeles
Nevada
New Hampshire
North Carolina
Northern Michigan
Northwest Texas
Rochester
Southern Virginia
Southwestern Virginia
Tennessee
Virginia
West Texas
West Virginia
Western North Carolina

Notes

PACIFIC

Pages 4-5

[1] Grace Cathedral Guidebook, 1980, p. 3.

[2] Ibid.

[3] Cathedral!, Issue 1, Vol. 1, Spring, 1991.

Page 6

[4] Lincoln, Joseph C., The Windows of Trinity Cathedral (Northland Press, 1973), p. 1.

[5] Ibid., p. 49.

[6] Arizona Episcopalian, Vol. 11, No. 4, June, 1991, p. 1.

Page 7

[7] Trinity Parish, San Jose, 1861-1961 (San Jose, 1961), p. 7.

[8] San Jose Mercury News, June 10, 1989, p. 14E.

[9] DeLisle, Joan C., The Trinity Windows (San Jose, 1977), p. 18.

[10] Ibid., p. 32.

Page 10

[11] Carey, the Rev. Grant, A Brief History of Trinity Cathedral Church (Sacramento, 1992).

[12] Ibid.

[13] Ibid.

Page 12

[14] Perkins, Louis L., A History of the Cathedral of St. John the Baptist (Portland, 1988), p. 18.

[15] Woodruff, Clinton Rogers, The Living Church, July 6, 1938, p. 147.

Page 13

[16] Barnes, C. Rankin, The Parish of St. Paul, Its First Hundred Years (St. Paul's Church, San Diego, 1969), p. 6.

[17] Ibid., p. 40.

[18] Gary, Ann, The Living Church, July 14, 1985, p. 9.

Page 15

[19] Hunt, Linda, The Cathedral on the Hill (Spokane, 1981), p. 29.

[20] Ibid., p. 30.

Page 16

[21] Whittaker, Thomas, Reminiscences of a Missionary Bishop (New York City, 1906), p. 381.

[22] A Brief History of the Cathedral of St. Mark.

EAST

Pages 18-19

[1] Wickersham, George W., The Cathedral Church of St. John the Divine (New York City, 1980), p. 5.

[2] Ibid., p. 12.

[3] Ibid., p. 40.

Page 20

[4] DeMille, George E., Pioneer Cathedral (Cathedral of All Saints, Albany, NY, 1972), p. 7.

[5] Ibid., p. 8.

[6] Ibid., p. 26.

[7] Ibid., p. 53.

[8] Welles, Edward Randolph, Guide Book to the Cathedral of All Saints (Albany, NY, 1938), p. 63.

Page 21

[9] Jones, John Philip, The Great Gray Spire (Quarier Printing Co., Syracuse, NY, 1985), p. 15.

[10] Ibid., p. 19.

[11] Ibid., p. 34.

[12] Ibid., p. 36.

Page 22

[13] Kendrick, Oliver, A Tour of the Cathedral, Hartford, 1976, p. 2.

[14] Ibid., p. 5.

[15] The Hartford Courant, May 26, 1992.

Page 23

[16] Godfrey, William C., On Historic Long Island (Kenneth R. Sanderson, Inc., Garden City, NY, 1971), p. 2.

[17] Ibid.

[18] Anglican Digest, Vol. 33, No. 4, July, 1991, p. 29.

Page 24

[19] Brinkler, Alfred, The Cathedral Church of St. Luke, A History of Its First Century (Portland: House of Falmouth, Inc.), p. 7.

[20] Ibid. p. 22.

[21] The Northeast, Vol. 118, No. 2, 1991, p. 1.

Page 25

[22] Powers, Katherine, The Cathedral Church of St. Paul—An Anniversary History, (Boston, 1987), p. 3.

[23] Ibid.

[24] Ibid., p. 11.

[25] Ibid., p. 20.

Page 27

[26] Trinity Cathedral, A Brief Historical Sketch (Newark, 1977), p. 6.

[27] Brown, Barton, The Voice Historical Supplement, May, 1986, p. 2.

[28] Trinity Cathedral, A Brief Historical Sketch (Newark, 1977), p. 6 .

[29] Brown, Barton, The Voice Historical Supplement, May, 1986, p. 3.

[30] Ibid.

[31] Trinity Cathedral, A Brief Historical Sketch (Newark, 1977), p. 12.

[32] Brown, Barton, The Voice Historical Supplement, May, 1986, p. 4.

Page 28
[33] Higgins, John S., From Corner Lot to City Block (Providence, 1972), p. 4.
[34] Ibid., p. 5.

Page 29
[35] Rothwell, Kenneth, A Goodly Heritage (Burlington, VT, 1973), p. 20.
[36] A History of St. Paul's Church, Burlington, VT, revised by J. Isham Bliss, 1899.
[37] Rothwell, Kenneth A., A Goodly Heritage, p. 21.
[38] Boyer, Donald, A Day Less Than a Thousand, New Life, January, 1974, p. 19.

Page 30
[39] Tomlinson, Juliette, "Thus out of small beginnings..." (Springfield: Christ Church Cathedral, 1972), p. 7
[40] Ibid., p. 13
[41] Ibid., p. 20
[42] Ibid., p. 34

SOUTHWEST

Page 34
[1] Cox, James R., Christ Cathedral, Salina (Nashotah, WI, unpublished, 1989), p. 7.

Page 37
[2] Sholty, the Rev. Ed, Cathedral Communitas, June, 1992, p. 3.
[3] Ibid.
[4] Ibid., p. 4.

Page 42
[5] Welles, Ferne M., A Church for the West Side (Grace and Holy Trinity Cathedral, Kansas City, MO, 1987), p. 7.
[6] Ibid., p. 37.

Page 43
[7] Phillips, Charles C., The First 150 Years (Mid-South Press, Inc., Shreveport, LA, 1990), p. 66.
[8] Ibid., p. 80.
[9] Ibid., p. 111.
[10] Ibid., p. 219.

MID ATLANTIC

Page 47
[1] Montgomery, Nancy, Guide to Washington Cathedral (National Cathedral Association, Washington, 1983), p. 33.
[2] Ibid., p. 35

Page 48
[3] Bethlehem Globe-Times, April 2, 1960.
[4] Ibid.

Page 49
[5] Lapitsky, Jacqueline, A History of Our Church (Harrisburg, Pa., 1976).

Page 50
[6] Handy, Victor D., A Short History of St. John's Church (Wilmington, 1947), p. 3.
[7] St. John's Parish, Wilmington, 1857-1957 (Wilmington, 1957), p. 19.
[8] Ibid., p. 40.

Page 51
[9] Preson, Dickson J., Talbot County, A History, 1983, p. 253.

[10] The Eastern Shore Churchman, Vol. I, No. 1, November, 1922.

Page 52
[11] Peabody, John N., Cathedral of the Incarnation (Baltimore, 1976), p. 36.
[12] Ibid., p. 37.
[13] Ibid.
[14] Ibid., p. 38.
[15] Ibid.
[16] Ibid., p. 43.

Page 53
[17] Woodruff, Clinton Rogers, The Living Church, April 20, 1938, p. 489.

Page 54
[18] Church News of the Diocese of Pennsylvania, January, 1917, p. 129.
[19] Davis, Steve, The Pennsylvania Episcopalian, February, 1992, Page A.

Page 55
[20] Mantle, Eric, Trinity and Pittsburgh (Pittsburgh, 1969), p. 6.
[21] Ibid., p. 9.
[22] Ibid., p. 22.

MID AMERICA

Page 58
[1] Scott, Benjamin Ives, and Neslund, Robert, The First Cathedral (The Cathedral of Our Merciful Saviour, Faribault, 1987), p. 6.
[2] Ibid., p. 13-14.
[3] Ibid., p. 23.
[4] Minnesota Missionary, December, 1941, p. 7.
[5] The First Cathedral, p. 168.

Page 59

6 Scott, Benjamin Ives, and Neslund, Robert, The First Cathedral (The Cathedral of Our Merciful Saviour, Faribault, MN, 1987), p. 121.

7 Schultz, Rima L., The Church and the City (Cathedral of St. James, Chicago, 1986), p. 69.

8 Ibid., p. 85.

9 Chicago's Cathedral 1861-1976 (Custombook, Inc., S. Hackensack, NJ, 1976), p. 3.

10 Schultz, Rima, The Church and the City, p. 194.

11 Ibid., p. 226.

Page 61

12 The Open Door, Vol. 47, No. 3, March, 1991, p.4.

Page 62

13 Brant, Gordon E., Hitherto Hath the Lord Helped Us (Eau Claire, 1958), p. 11.

14 Ibid., p. 34.

15 Brant, Gordon E., A Journey Through Christ Church Cathedral (Eau Claire, 1979), p. 5.

Page 63

16 Parker, Curtiss A., History of the Diocese of Fond du Lac, 1875-1925 (P.B. Haber, Fond du Lac, 1925), p. 31.

17 Ibid., p. 32.

18 Wagner, Harold E., The Episcopal Church in Wisconsin, 1847-1947 (Diocese of Milwaukee, 1947), p. 76.

19 Payne, Betty P., A Pilgrim's Guide to the Cathedral Church of St. Paul the Apostle (Fond du Lac), p. 2.

20 Ibid., p. 11.

Page 64

21 Stockton, Carl, Christ Church Cathedral Sesqui-centennial (Indianapolis, 1987), p. 6.

22 Ibid., p. 10.

Page 65

23 Bendixen, Sandra S., and Miller, Linda E., Historic St. Paul's Episcopal Church, Des Moines, Iowa, p. 22.

Page 66

24 The Living Church, June 19, 1988, p. 14.

25 Norton, Diane, A History of the Cathedral Church of St. Paul (Detroit, 1976), p. 9.

26 Ibid., p. 12.

Page 67

27 Wagner, Harold E., The Episcopal Church in Wisconsin, 1847-1947 (The Diocese of Milwaukee, 1947), p. 61.

28 Ibid., p. 62.

29 Delany, Selden P., All Saints' Cathedral, Holy Cross Magazine, June, 1913.

Page 68

30 Rodgers, Eugene L., And Then...a Cathedral (Christ Church Cathedral, St. Louis, 1970), p. 5.

31 The Altar and Reredos, Christ Church Cathedral (Eden Publishing House, St. Louis, 1960), p. 12.

Page 69

32 St. Peter's Pro-Cathedral Centennial, 1967, p. 9.

33 Ibid., p. 11.

Page 70

34 Martin, Charles W., The Church in the Middle of the Street (Omaha, 1952), p. 27.

35 Ibid., pp. 31-32.

36 The Nebraska Churchman, March, 1991, p. 1.

37 Woodruff, Clinton Rogers, The Living Church, July 6, 1938, p. 11.

Page 71

38 McNair, Mrs. A. W., Parish History of Gethsemane Cathedral (Fargo, ND, 1948), p. 1.

39 Ibid., p. 2.

40 North Dakota Churchman, February, 1890.

41 The Living Church, Oct. 22, 1989, pp. 9, 12.

42 The Sheaf, January, 1991, p. 3.

43 The Sheaf, May-June, 1991, p. 1.

Page 72

44 South Bend Free Press, Aug. 7, 1840.

Page 73

45 Woodruff, Clinton Rogers, The Living Church, July 6, 1938, p. 11.

46 Hehr, Russell Allon, The Windows and Chapel of Trinity Cathedral, p. 4.

Page 74

47 A Self-Guided Tour of The Cathedral Church of St. Paul, p. 1.

Page 75

48 Stark, Leland W.F., Calvary Cathedral in Sioux Falls, SD (The Cathedral Age, Spring, 1948)

Page 76

49 Barwell, Mike, Interchange, Vol. XXI, No. 2 (Cincinnati, Ohio), p. 2.

Page 77

50 Shutt, Philip L., The Cathedral Church of St. Paul, An Excursion Into History, (Springfield, IL, 1985), p. 6

51 Ibid., p. 9.

52 Ibid., p. 13 .

53 Ibid., p. 14.

54 Ibid.

Page 78
55 Western Michigan Episcopalian, Vol. 24, No. 7, September, 1990, p. 5.

Page 79
56 Jackson, Otis, St. Matthew's Cathedral (Laramie, Wyo., 1968), p. 38.
57 Ibid.
58 Ibid., p. 48.

SOUTHEAST

Page 82
1 The Episcopal Church Annual (Morehouse Publishing, Wilton, CT, 1991), p. 114.
2 Diocese, May, 1972, p. 8.
3 The Cathedral of St. Philip: A Pictorial History (St. Agnes Guild, Cathedral of St. Philip, Atlanta, 1988), p. 4.

Page 84
4 Rogers, Rebecca Pegues, How Firm a Foundation (Southern University Press, Birmingham, 1990), p. 1.
5 Ibid., p. 11.
6 Ibid., p. 60.
7 Gribbin, Emmet, A New/Old Cathedral for Alabama, Cathedral Age, Summer, 1982, p. 10.
8 How Firm a Foundation, p. 121.

Page 87
9 Parker, Dorothy Mills, Cathedral Age, Spring, 1984, p. 16.
10 Gordon, W. Stanley, A Short Architectural History of St. John's Cathedral Church (unpublished), p. 2.
11 Parker, Dorothy Mills, The Living Church, May 27, 1984, p. 6.

Page 88
12 Turner, Eleanor, The Windows of Christ Church Cathedral (Louisville, 1988), p. 3.

Page 89
13 Barr, Frances K., The Story of Christ Church, p. 2.
14 Swinford, Frances K. and Lee, Rebecca S., The Great Elm Tree (Faith House Press, Lexington, 1967), p. 13.
15 Barr, Frances K., The Story of Christ Church, p. 11.
16 Ibid., p. 22.
17 Ibid., p. 25.
18 Moody, William, The History of the Cathedral Domain (Diocese of Lexington, Lexington, KY, 1967), p. 21.
19 The Advocate, December, 1989, p. 7.

Page 90
20 Christ Church Cathedral (Christ Church Cathedral, New Orleans, LA), p. 2.
21 Ibid., p. 3.
22 Marrs, Norma Coons, A Lovely Old Cathedral, The Living Church, Aug. 29, 1982, p. 12.

Page 91
23 Wise, Sherwood W., The Cathedral Church of St. Andrew (Cathedral of St. Andrew, Jackson, MS, 1989), p. 19.
24 Ibid., p. 23.
25 Ibid., p. 159.
26 Ibid., p. 225.

Page 92
27 Bolger, Charles C., A History of the Cathedral Church of St. Luke and St. Paul, Radcliffboro (unpublished), p. 1.
28 Ibid.

Page 93
29 Ibid., p. 4.
30 Ibid., p. 4.
31 Jubilate Deo, Vol. XCVII, No. 4, April, 1991, p. 1.

Page 93
32 Parish Profile of Trinity Episcopal Cathedral (Trinity Cathedral, Miami, 1987), p. 3.

Page 94
33 Michaels, William M., St. Peter's Cathedral Centennial History (St. Petersburg, 1989).
34 St. Petersburg Times, Nov. 11, 1989.
35 Dobarganes, Mary S., The Stained Glass Windows of the Cathedral Church of St. Peter (St. Petersburg, 1989), p. 15.

Page 95
36 Hart, Georgia Herbert, Trinity Cathedral: A Thoughtful Study and Pocket Guide (Columbia, SC, 1978), p. 9.
37 Ibid., p. 6.

Photo Credits

Cover Quinta Scott
Page 1 Barron Krody
Page 14 M. A. Kinney
Page 15 Joel A. Moore Studio
Page 20 top, Edward Carpenter Brandow
bottom, Hay Photography
Page 21 Art Lange, artist
Page 22 Edna Baumann, artist
Page 24 top, Donald C. Patterson, artist
bottom, Arthur Towle
Page 25 David Zadig
Page 37 bottom, Debi Robinett
Page 40 Allan Stevens
Page 41 Richard DuFour, artist
Page 51 John Moll, artist
Page 58 Cheryl Younger
Page 60 Russell Phillips

Page 61 Robert E. Harris
Page 63 bottom, Carl Acker
Page 65 top, Ann Moore
Page 66 John Hartigan
Page 68 Quinta Scott
Page 70 Lynn R. Meyer
Page 74 Walker-Dauner Studio, Inc.
Page 76 bottom, Michael Barwell
Page 77 David E. Beatty
Page 79 Ted Edeen
Page 89 top, Fritz Cole
Page 90 Mike Posey